Prague

The Heart of Europe

*

▶
The Hradčany panorama. The best known view of the Vltava and Charles Bridge, the towers and roofs of the Lesser Town and the majestic Castle crowned by the cathedral, which gives ever new enchantment.

1 Agnes Convent
2 Bethlehem Chapel
3 Battle Field at the White Mountain, Star Summer Palace
4 U Kaštanu Tavern in Břevnov
5 Red Army Cenotaph
6 Carolinum
7 Emmaus Monastery
8 People's House in Hybernská
9 National Theatre
10 National Museum
11 former National House in Karlín
12 National Memorial on Žižkov Hill
13 New Town Hall
14 Kinský Palace
15 Memorial to Anti-Fascist Resistance in Kobylisy
16 Prague Castle
17 Old Town Hall
18 Staroměstské nám. (Old Town Square)
19 Tyl Theatre
20 Týn Church
21 Vyšehrad
22 Klement Gottwald Museum
23 Náprstek Museum
24 National Technical Museum
25 Jewish Museum
26 Museum of Decorative Arts
27 Military Museum (histor. part)
28 Military Museum (aircraft exhibition) at Kbely
29 Břevnov Monastery
30 Strahov Monastery
31 Clam-Gallas Palace
32 Tyrš House (Michna Palace)
33 Church of Our-Lady-of-the-Snows
34 Church of Our-Lady-Victorious (Prague Child Jesus)
35 Church of St Martin-in-the-Wall
36 Church of St Nicholas
37 Golden Well Restaurant
38 František Palacký Monument
39 Cubist building "At the Black Mother of God" (J. Gočár)
40 Cubist villas below Vyšehrad (Arch. Chochol)
41 House of the Squires of Kunštát
42 Faust House
43 House "At the Two Golden Bears"
44 Platýz Building
45 Portheim Gallery
46 Powder Tower
47 Old-New Synagogue
48 Vladislav Hall
49 Old Jewish Cemetery
50 Basilica of St George
HOLEŠOVICE
KARLÍN
ŽIŽKOV
VINOHRADY
VRŠOVICE
R. Vltava
Sports Hall
Julius Fučík Park of Culture and Rest
Fučíkova
K. Aksamit Stadium
U Uranie
Dělnická
Argentinská
Libeň Bridge
Park-Hotel
Fair Palace (under reconstruction)
Transport H.Q.
Vltavská
Bubenské nábřeží
Štvanice Island
Winter Stadium
Hlávka Bridge
Negrelli Viaduct
Brussels Restaurant
J. Šverma
Kl. Gottwald
Sokolovská
nám. Dr. Lyčky
Křižíkova
SS Cyril and Methodius's
Pernerova
St Peter's
City Museum
Music-Theatre (Karlín)
Vítězného února
E. F. Burian Theatre
Na poříčí
republiky
Prague Central Station
U Hybernů Exhibition Hall
Žižkov Hill (Vítkov)
Jan Žižka
Military Museum
Koněvova
Husitská
K. Havlíček
Kalininova
Central Council of Trade Unions
St Henry's
Vrchlický Park
Hlavní nádraží
Main Station
concourse of the Main Station
Theatre of Music
Esplanade Hotel
Jalta Hotel
Smetana Theatre
Federal Assembly
Hotel Wenceslas
Muzeum
National Museum
Rieger Park
F. L. Rieger
Bohemian Stadium
Olšany Cemetery
Public Cemetery
Želivského
Flora
Vinohradská
nám. Jiřího z Poděbrad
Jiřího z Poděbrad
STROJIMPORT Foreign Trade Corporation
Spejbl and Hurvínek Puppet Theatre
Vinohrady Theatre
Svatopluk Čech Park
Slezská
Šrobárova
nám. Míru
St Ludmila's
Nám. Míru
I. P. Pavlova
Wilhelma Piecka
Kotěra Villa
Francouzská
Lidových milicí
Vítězného února
Ruská
Kodaňská
Bělocerkevská
Třída SNB
St Wenceslas
nám. Sv. Čecha
Moskevská
Gröbe Villa
Havlíček Park
Bělehradská
Bohemians Sportsgrounds
Folimanka Hall
Klement Gottwald Bridge
Botič
Třída Sboru národní bezpečnosti
Slavia Stadium prim. Dr. V. Vacka (Slavia Praha IPS)
Gottwaldova

The big coat-of-arms of the capital city of Prague. Its basis is formed by the oldest emblem of the Old Town; the dual-tailed lion with the escutcheon of Slovakia on its chest behind the central helmet expresses the status of Prague as the capital city of the Czechoslovak Socialist Republic. The 47 pendants on the side helmets represent the towns and villages incorporated in Greater Prague.

Prague
The Heart of Europe

*

Text by
Bohumír Mráz

Photographs by
Pavel Štecha
and Pavel Vácha

HAMLYN

This edition published in 1988 by
Hamlyn Publishing Group, Bridge House,
69 Bridge Street, London Road,
Twickenham, Middlesex TW1 3SB,
and distributed for them by
Hamlyn Distribution Services

ISBN 0 600 55670 0

Printed in Czechoslovakia
2/99/73/51-01

Contents

Prague in the Heart of Europe

In the statue of Music (1907—1912) in the foyer of the National Theatre Josef Václav Myslbek expressed the lyrical musicality and harmonious melodiousness of the work of Bedřich Smetana, who immortalized Prague in his operas and symphonic poems.

Prague from Petřín Hill. The aesthetic effect of the
Prague terrain enhanced by its architecture was
determined by the steeply rising slopes of the Lesser
Town dominated by the Hradčany spur on the left bank
and the flat ground of the Old Town with the slowly
rising terraces of the New Town and of Vinohrady
on the right bank of the River Vltava.

Praga caput regni

Prague (Praha) lies only about 20 km north of the imaginary centre of Bohemia, at a location where the River Vltava provided suitable opportunity for fording. In prehistoric times an important trade route already led this way linking Eastern and Western Europe. When, at the end of the 9th century, the Přemyslids, princes of the tribe of Czechs, transferred their residence to Prague Castle protecting the ford across the Vltava, they laid the foundations of the future capital city of the state of Bohemia.

Prague became the residential city of the Bohemian rulers, and from 973 on, when the first bishopric was established here, it also became a Church centre. Those are the roots of Prague, the most important political, cultural and ideological centre of the Czech nation, as it has remained for a thousand years down to our own days.

"Holy" and "Royal" Prague

In the course of time the city acquired numerous honourable attributes that stress and enhance some of its characteristic features. The first name Prague was given was "holy". The reason for this was that its walls protected the sacred relics of martyrs, among whom special respect was attributed to the local martyrs, and, furthermore, from the earliest period, Prague was famous as a centre of advanced Christian culture.

Even before Prague became truly "royal" it was considered worthy of such a function. Lawrence of Montecassino, a monk, noted around 922 that "the city that is known as Prague is fit to be a royal residence and is the dwelling place of the rulers of those regions".

The first Czech King Vratislav I was crowned at Prague Castle in 1085. From that time on all the kings of the Přemyslid and Luxemburg dynasties took up residence in Prague, as did the Hussite King George of Poděbrady and, to begin with, also Vladislav of Jagiello. Twice, during the reign of Charles IV and Rudolph II, Prague became the capital and seat of the Holy Roman Empire. And even at times when it had long ceased to be the residential town of King or Emperor it managed to retain its dignity and truly "royal" majesty.

Prague from the Castle. The dozens of Gothic, Baroque and modern towers and spires of the Old and the New Town call to mind Prague's attribute of the City of a Hundred Spires.

The "Golden City of a Hundred Spires"

Prague acquired two other attributes. It became the "Golden City" under Emperor Charles IV when he had the Castle gates covered with new lead roofs that were thickly gilded "so that they may shine and glisten over a great distance during clear weather". He wanted to exemplify the great fame of his kingdom to the princes, rulers and nobility of the whole world, when they visited Prague Castle.

The label of "Golden Prague" appeared first in Rudolphinian literature and spread in subsequent centuries, long after the ravages of time had removed the gold from the roofs of Prague Castle. This epithet found its way into many local names, and visitors to Prague today are fond of sitting e.g. in the coffee-house "At the Golden Well" (U zlaté studně) in the Lesser Town (Malá Strana) to enjoy the magnificent view over the town. They can also get refreshments in the modern wine-cellar "At the Golden Serpent" (U zlatého hada) in Karlova street, or go for a glass of the famous Plzeň beer to the beer-cellar "At the Golden Tiger" (U zlatého tygra) in Husova street.

The attribute "The City of a Hundred Spires" came to be applied in the Baroque period, when Prague with its numerous Gothic towers and gateways was enriched with dozens of new cupolas, towers and spires. When in 1848 a count was taken of all Prague spires, it was shown that there were eighty-nine big ones, and over a hundred small ones. The name of the City of a Hundred Spires is, in other words, more than deserved.

More important than their number is the variety of their shapes and their location on Prague territory. The cupolas and towers of the churches help to shape the spatial and plastic image of the town with exceptionally refined taste, filling in empty spots in its overall composition and marking its dominant features of architecture and ground plan.

Allegory of the Vltava, a popular work by the Prague sculptor Václav Prachner on the fountain in the wall of Clam-Gallas Palace on Dr. Vacek Square (1812)

Prague — Gift of the River Vltava

The entire territory of the present city rests on a marl substratum. The River Vltava carved a broad and deep valley — the Prague basin — out of this marl plate made of mesozoic limestone formation. The river changed its course during centuries of history and in time of flood formed new arms and islands. The right bank of the Vltava rises gradually in contrast to the very impressive left bank. If we add the Vyšehrad Rock which opens up the Prague basin from the south and the transverse hills that protect it from the north, we have to acknowledge that the Vltava could not offer a more suitable site for a town.

The dramatic relief of the Prague region, the contrast of steep hills and land that descends in terraces determined the layout of the town, the location of squares, the direction of the streets and the siting of its main architectural features. Architects past and present have managed to put the advantages of this plastically modelled terrain to perfect use. In looking at the panorama of the city we admire the unique harmony of nature and architecture, which makes Prague stand out among the majority of other European cities.

Prehistoric and Romanesque Prague

The head of a "Bearded Man" on the Old Town side of the former Judith Bridge served as a reliable indicator of Vltava floods.

Legend and Reality

According to an old Czech legend Prague was founded by the wise Princess Libuše. Once — so the story runs — she stood on the walls of her residence at "Holy Vyšehrad" in the company of her retinue. Steeped in the spirit of divination she turned to the forest-clad hills on the far bank of the River Vltava and pronounced the words of her prophesy which appeared to foresee the coming destiny of the Czech metropolis: "I can see a vast city, whose fame reaches to the stars." The following day she ordered a new castle to be built on that site. Certain Bohemian chroniclers relate that this happened in the year 723.

Present-day archeological excavation at Prague Castle (Pražský hrad) has set the origin of the Castle in the second half of the 9th century. It was the tribe of the Czechs who selected a vacant site on a rocky spur above the Vltava for their new hill-fort. On this plastically shaped, uneven and rugged ridge they built a hill-fort that to this day is surprising for its size. The long and narrow settlement was divided into three parts adjusted to the terrain, the hill-fort proper with the dwelling of the chief and houses for his retinue, and two outer baileys.

In the western part of this site Prince Bořivoj, the first Prince to be attested historically, founded the first Christian church consecrated to the Virgin Mary. The unusual location of the church can be explained by the fact that it stood on the site of a former pagan shrine and was to symbolize the victory of the new Christian faith. Its foundations, built by the antique technique of spicatum walling, were found in 1950—1951. Bořivoj's single-naved church was pulled down soon after it was completed, and his son Prince Spytihněv erected a new church on the same site.

Soon after Prague Castle, another — the High Castle (Vyšehrad) — was founded on the opposite bank of the Vltava. Together they came to form the configuration typical of Prague that protected the settlement in the Prague basin and determined its new centres. From the Romanesque period on the history of the Czech nation unrolled in these two castles.

Libuše Prophesies the Glory of Prague, mosaic based on a drawing by Mikoláš Aleš in the vestibule of the Old Town Hall, made in 1937

The Prague Area before the Foundation of the Hradčany Hill-Fort

Archeological excavations have shown that people lived on the site of the present city and its surroundings already long before the foundation of the Prague hill-fort. In the early Stone Age primitive Man avoided the Prague basin, since the Vltava constantly changed its course and threatened the hunter and his prey with floods. He sought safer places higher up, and so we can find traces of him — stone tools and weapons — in a broad semi-circle to the west of Prague.

The Prague territory became permanently settled only in the Neolithic period. Peasants, who made linear pottery, founded several settlements, which archeologists have unearthed all over the area of Greater Prague today. The most important of these settlements lay to the north of Prague Castle, at present-day Bubeneč and Dejvice, and it is remarkable that they survived the Bronze and Iron Ages (the Únětice, barrow, Knovíz, and Bylany cultures) and in time grew larger and withstood the pressure of the Celts and the Germans. During the Roman period these were the most developed settlements on the territory of ancient Prague, with more than thirty iron-smelting ovens and involved in long-distant trade. When in the 5th century A.D. the Slavs occupied the Prague region and settled here as agriculturalists, they lived side by side with the original inhabitants, whose ethnic origin cannot be clearly determined. When the centre of settlement shifted to Prague Castle this other centre vanished.

Its place was taken by a Slavic settlement where the Lesser Town Square (Malostranské náměstí) is today, which came to form the core of the later Prague settlement below the Castle. The territory west of Prague Castle, inhabited from the Later Bronze Age on in view of its favourable location, was also densely settled by Slavs. The entire vicinity of today's Castle had, in other words, a long prehistory, the only exception being the Castle spur itself, which was not settled until the 9th century.

The Slavic hill-fort in Šárka Park west of Prague.
This territory was settled already in the Paleolithic period.

The St Wenceslas helmet of West European origin (10th century) in the St Vitus Treasure

Prague in the 10th Century — The First Historic Reports

We can discover from records left by Ibrāhīm ibn Ya'cūb, a Jewish merchant and diplomat in the services of the Khalif of Cordoba, what Prague looked like and what respect it enjoyed, when in 965 he passed through Bohemia on his way to Emperor Otto I. Firstly these historic records reveal that Prague initially only meant Prague Castle. For that alone could have had buildings of "stone and lime", which in kind, size, form and location were discovered by archeologists at the Prague hill-fort only quite recently.

From the 13th century onwards the term Castle (Hrad) also began to be applied to the settlement below the Castle. On the open space of Prague Castle enclosed by walls there stood three stone-built churches, the single naved Church of Our Lady built by Bořivoj and Spytihněv, Vratislav's Basilica of St George (sv. Jiří) and St Vitus' Rotunda, which Prince Wenceslas had built just before his martyr's death. The prince's palace was still a wooden structure, but in contrast with the log cabins for the other inhabitants of the fortress it already had stone foundations. While only insignificant fragments of the foundations of the first two churches have survived, we can today look at part of the apse of St Wenceslas' Rotunda in the underground parts of St Vitus' Cathedral as we go down to look at the tombs of the Kings of Bohemia.

The first Church of St Vitus (sv. Vít) was a circular building with a diameter of roughly 13 m and four horseshoe-shaped apses. It stood at Prague Castle until 1060, when it had to give way to a Romanesque basilica. When St Wenceslas and St Adalbert were buried here, it became a sacred reliquiary of the leading patron saints of Bohemia.

The worship of St Wenceslas, the first Přemyslid saint, did not make it possible for his tomb to be moved so that the architecture had to be adapted; the rotunda was supplanted by a Romanesque basilica, which then had to make way for a Gothic cathedral, but the tomb remained on its original site.

The first period when Christian culture flourished in Prague is linked with the person of St Wenceslas, who was murdered probably in 935. In a difficult international situation he set out to strengthen the state of Bohemia, both internally and in relation to neighbouring Germany, and his aim was to achieve a synthesis of the Old Slavonic and the Latin culture. The rotunda he built and the silver and gold buttons with ingrained and filigree ornaments found on Prague territory show that Prague tried, to some extent, to fulfil the role of the centre of the Great Moravian Velehrad. But the cult of the Saxon Saint Vitus and adherence to divine services in Latin reveal, on the other hand, that contacts with the Western cultural sphere were growing.

The tragic death of Prince Wenceslas turned this remarkable historic personality into a legendary hero. As a Christian martyr he became the dauntless patron saint of the nation and the symbol of the state of Bohemia. Before long he began to appear on the rulers seals and on Bohemian coins. The first Bohemian chorale was dedicated to St Wenceslas; the Crown of Bohemia was consecrated to him; his name was given to one of the main squares in Prague today, where there stands the equestrian statue of St Wenceslas, the work of sculptor Josef Václav Myslbek.

Ibrāhīm ibn Ya'cūb's report praises the advantages of the Prague market-place, but this is not localized in any detail. On the basis of the most recent excavations archeologists have placed this market-place in the immediate vicinity of the outer bailey of Prague Castle. The Old Town Square (Staroměstské náměstí) did not yet exist in the 10th century, and the area assumed the role of Prague's main market-place a whole century later.

Ibrāhīm visited Prague during the reign of Prince Boleslav I (c. 935—967), who assassinated his brother Wenceslas. The ruling Přemyslid dynasty made great use of marriages and important family members to establish contacts with other countries particularly in the south and east of Europe. Boleslav I's older daughter, Doubravka, married the Polish Prince Miezsko I, and became the first propagator of Christianity in

St Wenceslas, miniature in an initial
in the *Vyšehrad Codex* (1085). State Library
of the Czech Socialist Republic

Poland, while the younger Mlada persuaded the Pope in Rome to approve the establishment of the Prague bishopric in 973 and the foundation of the first convent of Benedictine nuns in Bohemia, St George's.

Prince Boleslav II (967—999) was the first who consolidated the Přemyslid reign by having the second most powerful family in the country, the Slavníks, assassinated in 995 and their stronghold (in Libice nad Cidlinou) destroyed. It was he who made Prague the capital city of his realm.

Prague in the 11th Century — Royal Vyšehrad

At the beginning of the 11th century the Polish ruler Boleslav the Brave took advantage of the disagreements between his cousins, the sons of Boleslav II. He seized Prague Castle and showed every intention of making Prague the centre of a great Bohemian-Polish state. The Prague Přemyslids Jaromír and Oldřich, however, drove the Poles from Prague Castle with the help of the King of Rome.

Prince Břetislav I (1034—1055), Oldřich's illegitimate son, consolidated the state of Bohemia, and also tried to take possession of Slovakia and Poland. He occupied Cracow and Gniezno and from there had the relics of St Adalbert brought to Prague and laid to rest in St Vitus Rotunda. He strengthened the fortifications of the Castle where new buildings for the Bishop, St Vitus' Chapter and St George's Convent, wre erected.

View of Vyšehrad from the Imperial Meadow

St Martin's Rotunda at Vyšehrad, the oldest of the three surviving Prague rotundas (end of 11th century, renovated 1878); the only remaining part of Romanesque Vyšehrad from the period when it flourished during the reign of the first King of Bohemia, Vratislav I.

His son Spytihněv II (1055—1061) paid the Pope annual dues of a hundred talents of silver and was accorded the right to wear a bishop's mitre. Spytihněv began to rebuild the main church in Prague, the Rotunda of St Vitus, into a Romanesque basilica and the work was completed by his brother Prince Vratislav II (1061—1092), who became the first King of Bohemia.

Vratislav was granted this title by Emperor Henry IV for his help in the struggle for the investiture of Pope Gregory VII, and in 1085 he had himself crowned in the bishop's church at Prague Castle. Before that he had begun to build up Vyšehrad as a new residence for the ruler, for, as a consequence of endless disputes with his younger brother Jaromír, the Bishop of Prague, he was unwilling to share his residence at Prague Castle with him.

He had a stone palace built at Vyšehrad and by its side the Basilica of SS Peter and Paul (sv. Petr a Pavel), in which he founded a chapter that was subordinate directly to Rome. The main church at Vyšehrad stood on the site where today we can see the Neo-Gothic building from the early 20th century. There probably was, furthermore, a basilica dedicated to St Lawrence. The cemetery rotunda consecrated to St Martin still stands there, after thorough restoration in 1878. With the older Church of St Clement, the Rotunda of St John the Evangelist and the building of the Mint, in which silver dinars were coined in the 10th century, Vratislav's Vyšehrad represented a dignified counterpart to Prague Castle.

At the intersection where the road linking the two castles crossed the old east-west trade route there grew up the settlement of Ungelt, with a new market-place and area in which foreign merchants enjoyed protection. This became the core of the future Old Town Square and the Old Town (Staré Město).

[21

The first King of Bohemia is associated with early Romanesque book painting in

Bohemia, the *Vyšehrad Codex* (Vratislav's Coronation Gospel). This magnificently illuminated manuscript (deposited in the State Library in the Clementium) ranks among the leading works of European Romanesque art with its wealth of subjects, magnificent colours and paintings. It was the main work produced in a workshop where many other illuminated manuscripts saw the light of day. It has never been settled whether the painters' workshop of the Master of the *Vyšehrad Codex* was actually situated at Vyšehrad or in the Benedictine Monastery at Břevnov, the first monastery in Bohemia, established by St Adalbert in 993. The same is true of the assumed existence of a Prague forge.

The Romanesque City

The last decade of the 11th century was a preparatory period in the development of Romanesque culture in Prague. In the 12th century this was clearly based on Western and Southern European stimuli and was under the influence of the universal Latin liturgy.

Prince Břetislav II (1092—1100) radically suppressed the surviving Slavonic liturgical tradition. The Slavonic monks of Sázava Monastery, which his father King Vratislav had generously supported even against the Pope's wishes, were driven away, and their place was taken by the Benedictines from the monastery at Břevnov.

The younger of Vratislav's sons, Prince Soběslav I (1125—1140), still resided at Vyše-

The Rotunda of St Longinus (second half of 12th century) in Na Rybníčku street in the New Town behind the Church of St Stephen

The interior of St George's Church at Prague Castle
(after 1142, remnants of older building periods in the 10th and 11th
centuries, restored 1888—1917 and 1958—1962).
A painting of the Heavenly Jerusalem (early 13th century)
is to be found on the vault of the choir. In front of the Baroque
stairways there are the tombs of Princes Vratislav II (right),
Boleslav II (centre), and Oldřich (left).

[23

hrad, where he continued building churches and devoted large sums of money to magnificent decorations and ornamentations of the halls in the Castle. At the same time he rebuilt Prague Castle in Romanesque style. Soběslav's large palace with mighty barrel vaulting can still be admired on the lowest floor of the Castle wing below Vladislav Hall.

Soběslav's sucessor, Vladislav II (1140—1172), transferred his residence permanently to Prague Castle. During his reign building activity greatly increased.

Prince Vladislav was a remarkable ruler, admired for his broad outlook and international contacts. He took part in the second crusade, from which he departed unexpectedly to visit Kiev and Constantinople. He joined Emperor Frederick Barbarossa in a campaign against the rebellious North Italian towns and was responsible for the speedy capture of Milan. The Emperor highly appreciated Vladislav's aid and endowed him in 1158 with the hereditary title of King. This was not acknowledged by his successor until Přemysl Otakar I, Vladislav's youngest son, was formally confirmed as King of Bohemia. This he achieved by means of political skill he was able to use in the complex situation which prevailed in Central Europe at the end of the 12th century and in the early 13th.

At the end of the Romanesque period Prague was an extensive settlement in the Vltava Basin with many small and large villages along both banks of the river between Prague Castle and Vyšehrad. The most important of the villages, apart from the settlement below Prague Castle, grew up around the market-place by the bend of the Vltava where the long-distance trade route led across the old fords. The ground plan of today's Old Town Square (Staroměstské náměstí) was basically fixed in the Romanesque period, which in many ways had equal influence on the layout of the network of streets in the future Old Town. The pattern followed the river whose course determined the natural location of the streets.

The winding little streets of the Old Town with their irregular pattern show that they came into existence by a natural process rather than deliberate human planning. As the surrounding land was raised at the end of the 13th century the original Romanesque houses became underground spaces, and remnants can be found in the cellars of the subsequent Gothic houses.

The Romanesque crypt of St George's Basilica (after 1142, vaulting renewed in the 17th century)

24]

Romanesque relief of the Crowning of the Virgin in St Anne's Chapel of the former St George's Convent (today houses the Collections of the National Gallery in Prague), culminating work of Romanesque sculpture in Bohemia in the first quarter of the 13th century, depicting tiny figures of Abbesses Mlada and Bertha by the throne of the Virgin, and Abbess Agnes and King Přemysl I on the side wings

The market-place on the site of the present-day Old Town Square was the centre of Romanesque Prague. This was where the main routes led to, here stood the Týn House for foreign merchants, and Jewish traders settled in its vicinity. But of greater importance for the founding and development of Prague was the Castle. This castle was already in existence when there was as yet no Old Town market-place, and when it became the residence of the Kings of Bohemia, this proved more important for the growth of the town, its economic prosperity and level of culture than the regular markets, which were held on the Old Town Square from the 12th century on.

Romanesque Prague was a fairly large town which comprised two castles with palaces, churches and chapels, four convents, more than thirty churches at the foot of the castles and seventy stone houses, not to mention the wooden houses that disappeared in later building construction. Across the Vltava led a stone bridge, Judith Bridge, which was named in honour of King Vladislav II's second wife, who was responsible for its construction. Prague had the second oldest stone bridge in Central Europe after Regensburg. The Lesser Town bridge tower survives, and its Renaissance sgraffito hides typical Romanesque ashlar walling. One of the most important reliefs of Prague Romanesque was set into the tower. It shows King Vladislav on the throne and a kneeling figure by his side who, in great likelihood, represents the builder of the bridge.

[25 Of the more than twenty Romanesque churches only two rotundas survive in the Old

The ground floor of the two-storey Romanesque house in Kaprova street in the Old Town (No. 16-I) below the building of the New Town Hall (second half of 12th century). The house was pulled down during clearance in 1909.

and the New Town today. The Rotunda of the Holy Rood (sv. Kříž) in Karolíny Světlé street and St Longinus' Rotunda (sv. Longin) in Na Rybníčku street. They are characteristic Bohemian Romanesque churches of a type that the Přemyslids adopted from the architecture of the Great Moravian Empire.

Remains of the original Romanesque structure can be found under the Gothic reconstruction of the Church of St Martin-in-the-Wall (sv. Martin ve zdi) in Martinská street, of St Wenceslas at Zderaz (sv. Václav na Zderaze) in Resslova street, and of the Basilica of St Peter (sv. Petr) in the street called Poříčí. The little Romanesque churches stood in the midst of isolated homesteads, villages or hamlets, denser settlement took place only in the vicinity of the Old Town market-place.

The only survivor of all the little churches on the left bank of the River Vltava is the basilica in the Premonstratensian monastery at Strahov, hidden now under the Baroque adaptations. Today the monastery serves as the Museum of National Literature (Památník národního písemnictví). Another important monastery belonged to the Knights of the Order of St John, known from the 16th century on as the Knights of Malta. It stood close to the stone Judith Bridge and few remnants have survived. The monastery was destroyed by the Hussites in 1419.

The building of Romanesque ecclesiastical architecture that survives in best condition is the Basilica of St George at Prague Castle. Its rich building history and numerous reconstructions and additions make it a most complex and interesting work of architecture. Traces of pre-Romanesque building stages have been found, but, in the first place, one becomes conscious of that special character of Bohemian Romanesque architecture, which differed from that of Western basilicas by its smaller scale and simplicity. On the vaulting of the choir and in the southern nave can be seen remnants of Romanesque frescoes from the first quarter of the 13th century. In front of the crypt one's attention is attracted by three stone tombs, on the right that of Prince Vratislav II, the founder of the church, in the middle Boleslav II, the founder of the Convent, and, to the left, his son Oldřich.

In the adjacent St George's Convent (Jiřský klášter) — originally Romanesque, rebuilt in Gothic style — the National Gallery exhibits its collection of Bohemian Gothic, Renaissance and Baroque art. In St Anne's Chapel in the northern wing of the cloisters a fitting place was reserved for the most important relief of Romanesque Prague, in which the two builders of the convent, the first Abbess Mlada and Abbess Bertha, kneel below the throne of the Crowned Madonna. Abbess Bertha was responsible for the rebuilding of the convent after a fire in 1142. On the wings we can see the figures of King Přemysl Otakar I praying and his daughter Abbess Agnes, who had the convent church decorated with mural paintings and donated this relief. The chapel is the last resting place of the Abbesses of St George's beginning with Mlada.

One of the most remarkable features of Romanesque Prague were its stone houses. The

The Romanesque Palace of the Squires of Kunštát (c. 1200) in Řetězová street in the Old Town (No. 222-I), one of the most magnificent secular buildings in Romanesque Prague

first of these were discovered at the beginning of our century during slum clearance operations in the Old Town, and since then dozens of others have been found, so that today we know of some seventy. Most of them exist only up to their ground floor level in the present cellars of Gothic houses. They had a variety of ground plans, were covered by cross vaulting and rested on a central column. They did not form continuous rows but existed as separate units accessible from a yard.

A clear picture of the construction of Prague Romanesque houses can be derived from the largest building, which has survived in Řetězová street and which belonged to the Squires of Kunštát in the later Middle Ages. Today it is used for exhibition purposes. Remnants of mural paintings reveal how luxuriously the interiors were decorated. Some such murals were accidentally discovered when one of the Romanesque houses was demolished. The paintings represented figures of the monarchs.

To say that Romanesque Prague was truly a city is to exaggerate slightly. It must be realized that Prague was at the time not a town in the medieval sense of the word, for it possessed no town charter, no administration of its own nor any walls. There was no continuous built-up area, it only provided the framework and focal points of the subsequent Gothic town.

The figure of a King on the mural painting (c. 1250) in a demolished house of the Romanesque period in Platnéřská street in the Old Town shows the advanced culture of the Prague settlement below the Castle in that time. Museum of the City of Prague

Gothic Prague

Stone Virgin, house sign from the years 1450—1460. Museum of the City of Prague

The Foundation of the Gothic Town

When Přemysl Otakar I's son Wenceslas I (1230—1253) ascended the royal throne a new era seemed to open up. One epoch had come to an end, a new one began to emerge. The place of early feudalism with its natural economy was taken by developed feudalism, requiring a far more differentiated society, where preference was given to rent in money, thus the building of towns was encouraged.

These social and economic changes are reflected best in art. The Romanesque style was

The Cloister Court of the Convent of the Blessed Agnes in the Old Town of Prague, originally the dormitory of the Poor Clares, reconstructed in 1963—1964 according to a design by Joef Hizler based on finds from the 13th century

replaced by Gothic. Gothic Prague grew up — literally and figuratively — on top of Romanesque Prague, the royal town became the residential town of the monarch of Bohemia. While Přemysl Otakar I had managed to ensure the leading position of the state of Bohemia and with it its metropolis, his son Wenceslas I established the Gothic town within the framework of the multi-national medieval Roman Empire and did so by having the Romanesque settlement on today's Old Town surrounded by walls. Inside he ordered new quarters to be built on empty ground, and he granted the inhabitants a royal Charter.

Wenceslas' son Přemysl Otakar II complemented his father's work by founding what today is the Lesser Town (Malá Strana), whereby a second Gothic town arose on Prague territory. He was the first King of Bohemia to lay claims to and win the imperial Crown, but he paid for his ambitions with his life at the Battle on the Marchfield in 1278. As rival to the King of Rome he was opposed there by an alliance of the Habsburgs and Hungarians supported by the Pope. During a favourable international situation in the early 14th century his son Wenceslas II, for a short time, acquired the Crowns of Poland and Hungary for the Přemyslids, but with the assassination in 1306 of Wenceslas III — the last male heir of the Přemyslid dynasty — the first Bohemian royal house suddenly became extinct. All the achievements of the Přemyslids were wasted, and Prague, previously the residence of a king of three lands, once again became witness to destructive struggles for power.

The town walls built after 1231 under King Wenceslas I enclosed the Old Town to the south and east in places where today run Národní, Příkopy and Revoluční streets. The wall was a double one with two moats. Its existence is today symbolized by the name of one of the main thoroughfares in the centre of Prague linking Wenceslas Square (Václavské náměstí) with Republic Square (náměstí Republiky). Later, around the middle of the 13th century, a single wall was erected in the bend of the River Vltava so that the town was fortified on all sides. Since these fortifying walls stood further away from the river there was room enough on the riverbanks for timber markets, mills and ironworks, which put the water power to use and formed a picturesque and lively backyard to the medieval town.

The main stretch of walls to the east and south facing the later New Town was fortified with thirteen towers and gateways, some of which were not finished until the second half of the 13th century. All that remains of the fortifications of the Old Town is the Powder Tower (Prašná brána) built in Late Gothic decorative style towards the end of the 15th century on the site of an Early Gothic gateway from the first quarter of the 13th century. Its present form is the result of purist Neo-Gothic restoration in 1875—1886. The remains of the original stone bridge across the moat that divided the Old Town from the New were discovered by archeologists during the construction of Prague Metro (the underground) and can be viewed in the entrance lobby to the Můstek Metro station.

The Gothic walls made use of the advantages offered by the terrain, and for that reason they enclosed the older Romanesque settlement unevenly. To the south, for example, they separated the village of St Martin from its church, which thus found itself in the walling of the fortifications — hence the name St Martin's-in-the-Wall (sv. Martin ve zdi). To the south-east, east and north there remained large open spaces inside the walled area, waiting to be settled. This took place at the same time as the building of the fortifications.

In 1232—1234 the surveyor and builder Eberhard, later Master of the Royal Mint, founded the Gall Town (Havelské město), a settlement on a regular ground plan around an elongated and rectangular market-place. They placed the parish church of St Gall (sv. Havel) and the royal court of law in its centre. Here German colonists built Early Gothic houses with mighty stone towers, remnants of which have recently been discovered. King Wenceslas I granted the settlement a royal Charter giving the inhab-

The Church of St Saviour in Agnes' Convent (c. 1280), its later part built in the dignified style of French Gothic of the Paris region

itants the right to self-administration — supervised by the Royal Magistrate — and so the town came to be known as the town by St Gall's.

The immense market-place called the New Market (in contrast with the Old Market on the Old Town Square) stretched between what is today the Coal Market (Uhelný trh) and the Fruit Market (Ovocný trh), and its original layout can still be observed despite later building construction. In the 14th century the market-place was split in two by two rows of merchants' stalls. The Baroque period saw the building of a monastery at St Gall's, Neo-Classicism added a theatre building in its midst and at the end of the 19th century they located here — in a most insensitive manner — the bulky building of the Town Savings Bank (today the Klement Gottwald Museum).

The Gothic atmosphere of the Gall Town can be felt most strongly in the arcades of Havelská street with their cross vaulting on stone ribs. Such arcades originally surrounded the entire market-place. They remained Gothic in the proportions of the narrow façades of the houses, built on deep, typically medieval building lots. During the Renaissance and Baroque periods artistic features alone were added to the façades. To the north, the Gall Town settlement centred around the Church of St Benedict, no longer in existence, to which the Order of the Teutonic Knights moved from Poříčí around 1233 and set up a monastery.

A far more important centre arose at the northern end of the Gothic walls near the

R. Vltava where Princess Agnes, the sister of King Wenceslas I, built two associated Franciscan convents after 1234, one for monks and the other for nuns, and she herself became the first Abbess there. The Blessed Agnes, a friend of St Clare, with whom she corresponded, was a personality of European significance at the beginning of the Gothic period. Her name is linked both with the origin of the first Franciscan monastery in Central Europe and the foundation of the only knightly Order of Crusaders with a Red Star in Bohemia. In 1252 this Order was granted a permanent site near the stone bridge where today stands the Baroque Monastery and Church of St Francis (sv. František), whose cupola forms such a characteristic feature in the panorama of Prague.

The former Convent of the Blessed Agnes (Anežský klášter) is one of the most precious monuments in Prague since it was the first Gothic building in Bohemia. In Germany

Capital of the pillar of the triumphal arch in the Church of St Saviour with little sculptured heads of the royal dynasty of the Přemyslids, the founders of the monastery (middle of 13th century)

The Old-New Synagogue, the oldest in Europe and the most important monument of the former Prague ghetto, a precious example of the Early Gothic style in Prague (second half of 13th century). The Gothic brick gables date into the 14th century.

The original Early Gothic portal of the Old-New Synagogue with finely carved ornaments. This is the oldest surviving architectonic portal in Prague (second half of 13th century).

and in Bohemia the Gothic style was applied a century later than in France where it originated. The earliest Gothic buildings in Prague were constructed by a Cistercian masonic lodge from Burgundy. This should be taken into account when we find the noble shapes of classical Gothic architecture of the Paris region in later parts of the Convent of the Blessed Agnes, completed in the second half of the 13th century, and in the Church of St Saviour (sv. Salvátor). Today the entire grounds of Agnes' Convent are administered by the National Gallery, which, after extensive restoration and adaptation, has installed its Collection of 19th Century Czech Painting here.

The foundation of the Gothic town by Wenceslas I was a stimulus for new "town" Orders—the Dominicans and Franciscans (Minorites) even inside the original Old Town. The Dominicans resided until the Renaissance period near the Church of St Clement (sv. Kliment), close to the Bridge. (The church and monastery were demolished during the Jesuit construction of the Clementinum.) The Franciscans were established near the Church of St James (sv. Jakub) behind Ungelt. Nothing has survived of its early Gothic period. Its present appearance dates from Baroque adaptations of the Gothic nave and aisles in the 14th century, and the monastery cloisters date from the same period.

The Foundation of the Lesser Town

The creation of the Gothic town on the right bank of the Vltava further stressed the exigency of the problem of dealing with the heterogeneity and scattered character of the Romanesque settlement on the left bank below the Castle. The matter was solved in 1257 by Wenceslas' son Přemysl Otakar II (1253—1278) in the radical manner typical of this monarch. The existing Bohemian inhabitants were forced to move into a village in the close vicinity, and in their place he summoned colonists from North Germany, who, with his consent, founded a new Gothic town laid on a regular ground plan that paid no regard — apart from important ecclesiastical buildings — to the existing houses.

The centre was formed by a large rectangular market-place, today's Lesser Town Square, with a new Gothic parish Church of St Nicholas (sv. Mikuláš). The town was surrounded by Gothic stone walls which linked up with the Castle, the Bishop's Court and a monastery of the Order of St John by the stone bridge. The town was administered according to Magdeburg Law and called the New Town of Prague (Nové Měs-

The golden St Wenceslas Crown of the Kings of Bohemia, commissioned by Charles IV for his coronation in 1347 and made out of the original Přemyslid Coronation Jewels. It has 91 gem-stones and 20 pearls. From 1358 on it adorned the golden reliquary bust of St Wenceslas. The Orb and Scepter with figural decorations date from the second half of the 16th century. Crown Chamber of St Vitus' Cathedral

The golden Coronation Cross inlaid with antique cameos from the third quarter of the 14th century. Part of the St Vitus Treasure

to). It was not until Charles IV founded his New Town on the right bank of the Vltava in 1348 that this part was re-named the Lesser Town of Prague (Menší Město).

Thus at the beginning of the Gothic period a situation arose that was characteristic of the history of Prague in contrast with many other towns: Prague became a twin town. Since the two Prague towns lay close to one another, their special conditions had to be catered for and reconciliation was necessary when interests conflicted.

The Lesser Town of Prague (today's Malá Strana) was not, at the time of its foundation, an entirely equal partner of the Old Town. Its livelihood depended on Prague Castle below which it stood and its powers were limited by both the monasteries which administered a large section of the territory and the growing pressure on the part of the Old Town citizens. They laid claims not only to the entire Bridge, but to the Lesser Town banks and the foot of Petřín Hill.

All that remains of the Gothic Lesser Town is the ground plan and layout of today's Lesser Town Square with four streets running towards the Bridge and three gateways with towers, which have long been pulled down. But in the courtyard of the building at the corner of the Lesser Town Square and Karmelitská street (Nos. 271-272), which in the 15th century for a short time was the town hall, one finds remnants of the original wall towers from the period of Přemysl Otakar II. The Gothic parish Church of St Nicholas, consecrated in 1283, gave way, in the 18th century, to the Baroque church of the same name. The same is true of the Augustinian monastery with the Church of St Thomas (sv. Tomáš). This monastery was founded in 1285 by King Wenceslas II in memory of his father Přemysl Otakar II, but the church was not completed until after the death of Emperor Charles IV in 1379.

◀
The apse of the choir of St Vitus' Cathedral at Hradčany. The building was begun by Mathieu d'Arras (1344—1352) and continued by Peter Parler (1356—1399)

The bust of the first architect of St Vitus' Cathedral, Mathieu d'Arras, in the triforium, dated 1374—1385

The Growth of Gothic Prague under the Last Přemyslids

King Wenceslas II (1278—1305) tried to carry out the grandiose idea of Přemysl Otakar II to raise Prague to the status of capital city of a vast Central European empire; first he consolidated conditions in the Kingdom of Bohemia after years of decline, caused by the Brandenburgs, famine and the pest. When the ruling dynasty in Poland weakened, in 1300 he married the daughter of the Piast King and had himself crowned with the Royal Crown of Poland at Gniezno. In the following year the royal House of the Arpads became extinct, and he won the crown of Hungary for his son Wenceslas III. Then he could afford to have himself celebrated by German Minnesängers in his palace at Prague Castle — reconstructed in Gothic style by Přemysl Otakar II. They sang and glorified him for having established without battles an empire that stretched from sea to sea.

The power of the Přemyslids did not last long, for the Pope put a member of the French House of Anjou on the throne of Hungary. The last Přemyslid, Wenceslas III, was assassinated during a campaign against the rebellious Poles in 1306, a mere year after he ascended the throne. The Luxemburgs then followed up the policy of expansion initiated by the Přemyslids. The Luxemburgs were the second royal dynasty of Bohemia; they proved more successful and their acquisitions were of more lasting validity.

King Wenceslas II benefited from the backing of the Church, in particular the Cistercian Order, in his home policy opposing the nobility who had caused his father's fall. The Cistercians were the main Order who propagated and spread Gothic architecture.

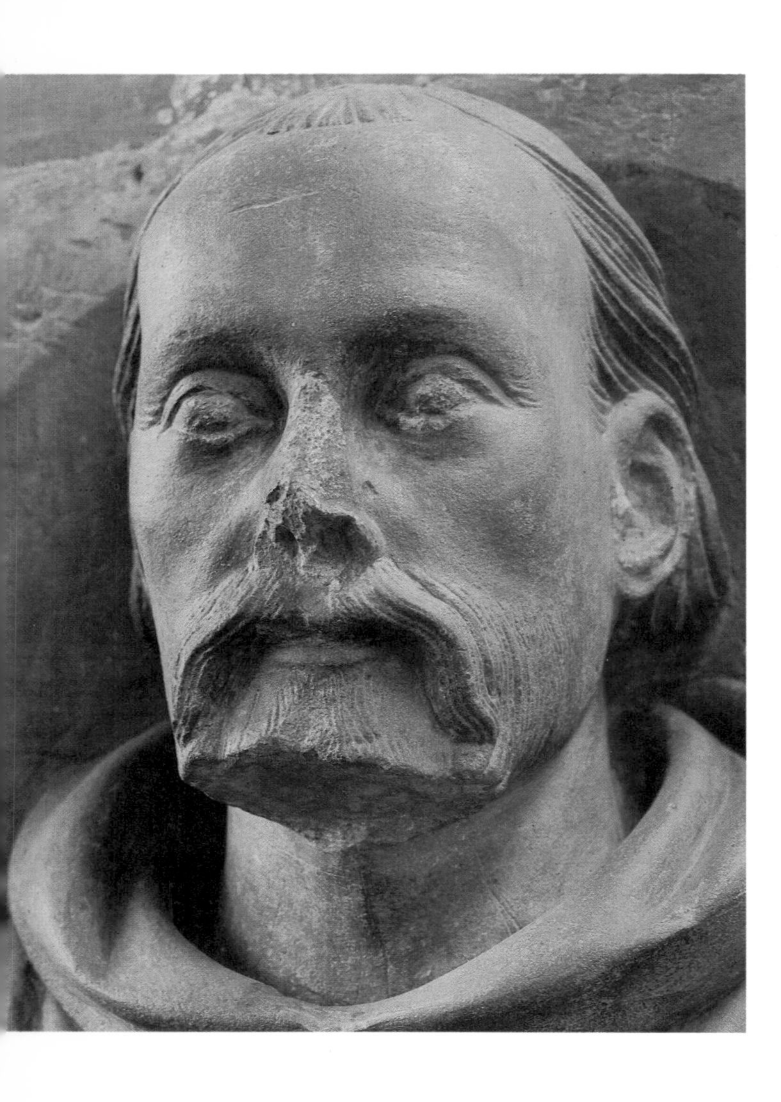

Portrait of the second builder of St Vitus' Cathedral, Peter Parler, likewise in the triforium (1374—1385)

▶
The interior of the choir of St Vitus' Cathedral, covered with net vaulting by Peter Parler in 1385

Wenceslas founded a monastery and a magnificent Gothic church for the "grey monks". It was built at Zbraslav, some ten kilometres from Prague upstream on the site of a hunting lodge, and this was to be the last resting place of the Kings of Bohemia. The church and the monastery were destroyed by the Hussites, and today we can find in its stead a beautiful château, adapted before the First World War from a Baroque monastery. Its interior was fitted out in modern manner, and the National Gallery in Prague has installed its Collection of Czech 19th and 20th Century Sculpture there.

During the reign of Wenceslas II, towards the end of the 13th century and particularly after a fire in 1291, the two Prague towns were given a Gothic appearance. The older Romanesque buildings — many still wooden — of the Old Town and the Lesser Town gradually gave way to new tall Gothic houses with high gables and roofs set close together in a row along the street or enclosing a square with continuous arcades sheltering tradesmen's workshops and merchants' stalls.

The most radical changes in the Old Town occurred in the last decades of the 13th century. To protect the town from floods the level of the ground was artificially raised by an average of 2—3 metres. Romanesque Prague thus symbolically and literally found itself in the cellars of Gothic Prague. Early Gothic builders laid the foundations of the future development, and the new ground level they established has remained the same to the present days with few exceptions. That the Old Town was able to afford the cost of raising the ground points to its economic prosperity. Towards the end of the 13th century there already existed the first organization of craftsmen, a brotherhood which later developed into a guild. The growth of trade led to the setting up of new specialized market-places and the codification of rights and duties of foreign merchants. Markets were held in the Týn Yard, a walled area in the Old Town.

St Wenceslas' Chapel in St Vitus' Cathedral, built by Peter Parler in the years 1362—1364. On the lower parts of the walls inlaid with Bohemian semi-precious stones there are Gothic mural paintings with scenes of the Passion in *The St Wenceslas Legend*, the work of the Master of the Litoměřice Altarpiece in the early 16th century.

The Prague patriciate grew wealthier as the result of participation in mining silver, trade in precious metals and money-lending, and their political consciousness and ambitions for power grew accordingly. In 1296 they petitioned the King to permit them to build a town hall and to employ a Town Clerk. Wenceslas II approved only the Clerk. When the Přemyslids died out, the patriciate took an active part in the struggle for power among the claimants to the royal throne of Bohemia.

At that time there stood more than twenty churches in the Old Town. Town life was centered around four squares — the Old Town (Staroměstské), the Gall (Havelské), the Goat (Kozí) and the Virgin Mary (Mariánské, now Dr. Vacek) Squares, and in a number of streets which were reserved for specialized craftsmen: this sometimes gave the streets the name surviving to the present, e. g. Sweetbread-Makers (Celetná), Armourers (Platnéřská) and Joiners (Truhlářská).

At that time, too, around 1287, the town privileges were unified, and even the Gall Town submitted to the unified town jurisdiction. Close to the Old Town walls lived groups of inhabitants with varying legal status. They included Germans, Italians, Jews, noble-

Statue of St Wenceslas in St Wenceslas' Chapel in St Vitus' Cathedral, 1373, probably made by Henry Parler, Peter's nephew

men, various Church organizations, free people and serfs, and introducing order into their complicated interrelations was a long-term process. In the end a town statute emerged and leading town authorities were established: a Royal Magistrate, who, with the help of twelve counsellors, was named by the King to be in charge of the jurisdiction and the administration of the Old Town.

King Wenceslas II made Prague famous for its new silver coinage, the Prague Groschen, which soon became popular among the merchants in neighbouring countries. His attempt to make Prague a university town came to nothing when the Bohemian aristocracy refused consent. It was not until Wenceslas II's grandson, Emperor Charles IV, used the propitious international situation that Wenceslas II's ambitious plan was realized.

The development of Prague during the reign of the last Přemyslids brought problems of a different kind — a striking increase in the number of German inhabitants. By way of feedback this led to the rapid growth of Czech national awareness, which appeared most clearly in literature. In the *Dalimil Chronicle* the nationality problem arising from the conflicting interests of the Bohemian gentry and the German townspeople runs like a thread through the entire book.

St George and the Dragon by the brothers George and Martin of Cluj, 1373. A copy of the statue stands on the third courtyard of the Castle, the original is in the National Gallery.

[45

Mosaic of the Last Judgment on the southern Golden Gate of Prague Cathedral made by Venetian artists according to a Bohemian pattern and from Bohemian glass in 1371. The Patron Saints of Bohemia and Charles IV with his fourth wife, Elizabeth of Pomerania, kneel below Christ.

The Adoration of the Kings in the Saxon Chapel of St Vitus' Cathedral, c. 1370, Bohemian High Gothic mural painting

The Succession of the Luxemburgs

—

The Foundation of the Hradčany District

After the Přemyslid dynasty died out, four years of turmoil followed and the towns were laid waste while the Habsburgs, for the first time and as yet unsuccessfully, tried to gain access to the throne of Bohemia. Then the young, 14-year-old John of Luxemburg fought and forced his way to Prague in 1310. He was the husband of Elizabeth, daughter of Wenceslas II. John himself was the son of the Holy Roman Emperor Henry of Luxemburg, and his relatives included the Kings of France as well as the abbots of Cistercian monasteries who negotiated his summons to Bohemia and placed high hopes in the new King. Even though they were probably disappointed in the end, his reign did bring considerable prosperity to the Kingdom of Bohemia and to Prague itself.

John of Luxemburg was one of the last great medieval knights and Edward III of England even called him the "Crown of Knightdom". He tried to concentrate all power in his hands and to rule as absolute king, but the Bohemian nobility did not allow him to do so. He had to concede their involvement in home policy while he concerned himself primarily with international relations. On the whole his foreign policies proved successful, and he added Silesia, Upper Lusatia and the Cheb region to the Kingdom of Bohemia. Since King John became involved in almost every political event and war in Europe, it came generally to be assumed that "without the aid of the Lord and the King of Bohemia nobody will ever succeed in anything".

Bohemia, however, was forced to finance King John's foreign adventures. The King spent little time in the country and at Prague Castle, and when he did so, it was usually simply to collect new funds. The people of Prague won various privileges when they showed willingness to pay, and in 1338 John permitted them to build a town hall. This was the culmination of the Prague citizens' efforts to gain political emancipation. The town hall became a visible symbol of the town's autonomy which pushed the Royal Magistrate into the background. That same year the people of the Old Town purchased the Wölflin House on the corner of the Old Town Square. Gradually they adapted the interior and enlarged it to house the counsellors and, in the second half of the 14th century they erected a square tower and a chapel with an oriel window. In 1341 the King allowed them to elaborate a new legal code, and he acknowledged the

Prince Břetislav I on the tomb in the Choir Chapel of St Vitus' Cathedral. Together with five other tombs of Přemyslid princes this is the work of the Parler masonic lodge after 1373.

Master Theodoric, St Elizabeth, panel painting, before 1365

legal sovereignty of the Old Town over the other towns. In this manner Prague acquired the exclusive status of "Mother of Towns".

During the reign of John of Luxemburg the Old Town improved its facilities and its external appearance. The streets were paved, and more attention was paid to cleanliness. The last remnants of Romanesque Prague gave way to ostentatious and comfortable Gothic houses whose tall tripartite façades were decorated with ledges and niches. By that time almost all streets and squares of the Old Town were already in existence. Building had begun on the Franciscan Church of St James (sv. Jakub, 1316), the northern nave of St Castulus' (sv. Haštal) was completed, and thanks to the last bishop of Prague, Jan of Dražice, a remarkable single naved Church of St Giles (sv. Jiljí) was built, which was the third largest church in Prague in the period prior to Charles IV.

Jan of Dražice was prominent in Prague's political and cultural life during the reign of John of Luxemburg. He encouraged the new Gothic art, with which he had become

Votive panel of the Archbishop Jan Očko of Vlašim, before 1371. In the upper strip: Charles IV, St Wenceslas and St Sigismund by the side of the Virgin and Child enthroned. Below: the kneeling donor with the four Patron Saints of Bohemia

[49

acquainted during his long attendance at the papal court in Avignon. He had his bishop's palace in the Lesser Town rebuilt according to the French pattern and decorated it with magnificent decorations in painting and sculpture culminating in a number of bronze statues of Prague bishops, his predecessors in office. Unfortunately, the palace and its artistic decorations were destroyed during the Hussite upheavals together with the Cartusian church and monastery at Smíchov which King John built and richly decorated.

C. 1320 the Burgrave of Prague Castle, Berka of Dubá, founded a third Prague town along the old road from Pohořelec to the Castle and called it Hradčany. It was to be a town of serfs and therefore less significant than the two older towns. Originally it included only the present Hradčany Square (Hradčanské náměstí) and the area to the west of it towards the present U kasáren street. But by the second half of the 14th century it had spread to Pohořelec, Úvoz and Nový Svět (New World). The character and appearance of Hradčany was for a long time determined by its dependence on the Castle. Only in the Renaissance period, in 1598, did Emperor Rudolph II raise it to the status of "royal town".

During John's reign there were increasing cultural and artistic contacts between Prague and Western Europe, particularly Paris. The King of Bohemia himself had been educated in France, was related to the royal family of the Capets, and was completely at home in Paris. A magnificent example of the stimulating influence of French and

The single-naved Gothic Church of St Apollinarius in the New Town. It was founded by Charles IV for the Chapter from Sadsko after the middle of the 14th century. Re-Gothicized by Josef Mocker in 1897

English art on Bohemian book illustrations is the *Passional* of the Abbess of St George's Convent, Chunegunda, daughter of Přemysl Otakar II. This outstanding work of Gothic mysticism, like the surviving remnants of architecture, sculpture and mural painting, shows how the reign of John of Luxemburg was, in every respect, a preparation for the subsequent glorious rule of Charles IV. At that period Prague lived through the most famous and most magnificent chapter of its history.

The Building of the Gothic City during the Reign of Emperor Charles IV

The personality and work of Charles IV embodied and enhanced the advantages, positive mental qualities and abilities, the endeavours and longings of many generations of his predecessors. He was a Luxemburg after his father John, the grandson of a Holy Roman Emperor; he was related to the French royal family and the Dukes of Brabant, and he considered himself a descendent of the founder of the Holy Roman Empire, whose name he bore. On his mother's side he was a Přemyslid, and he proudly

The fortifications of Vyšehrad, with Karlov behind them

acknowledged his Czech origin, and he regarded St Wenceslas, the first Přemyslid saint and patron of Bohemia, as an ideal ruler and Christian.

He was christened Václav (Wenceslas), and he did not begin to use the name Karel (Charles) until after his confirmation adopting it from his godfather King Charles V of France. He was for his time an exceptionally well educated ruler, he spoke French, Latin, Italian, German and Czech and possessed a quite exceptional appreciation of the significance and value of culture and the arts. He generously supported development of the arts, without neglecting agriculture, manufacturing and trade. There was no one to rival him in statesmanship and diplomatic skill. In his youth he was highly courageous like his adventurous father, but he preferred to extend the frontiers of his kingdom with the aid of money or by political marriages. He was talented and strong willed but could wait with patience and pursue with perseverance a goal he set himself. And unlike any of his Přemyslid ancestors he was lucky: destiny or — as he himself was convinced — God's will was on his side. He was the first King of Bohemia to win the Imperial Crown without resorting to battle. He managed to enlarge the state of Bohemia by peacefully acquiring the remaining Silesian principalities, Upper Lusatia, estates in the Upper Palatinate, the Meissen region, Foitland, and Brandenburg.

The reign of Charles IV brought to Prague great changes in scope and significance. Prague became the residential town of the King of Rome (1346) and the Emperor (1355) and the capital city of the Holy Roman Empire. In 1333, during the reign of his father, Charles began rebuilding Prague Castle, which had not been inhabited since a fire in 1303. When in 1344 he managed to have the bishopric of Prague raised to archbishopric, he solemnly laid the foundation stone of the Gothic Cathedral of St Vitus, which replaced the Romanesque basilica. In 1348 Charles IV founded the University of Prague, the first in Central Europe, and that same year the New Town of Prague, which encompassed within the walls a vast area between Poříčí and Vyšehrad (which he rebuilt in great splendour) with all the old Romanesque homesteads and the land between them. In 1357 he had a new stone bridge built in the place of the Romanesque Judith Bridge, which had been torn away during a flood in 1342. Final-

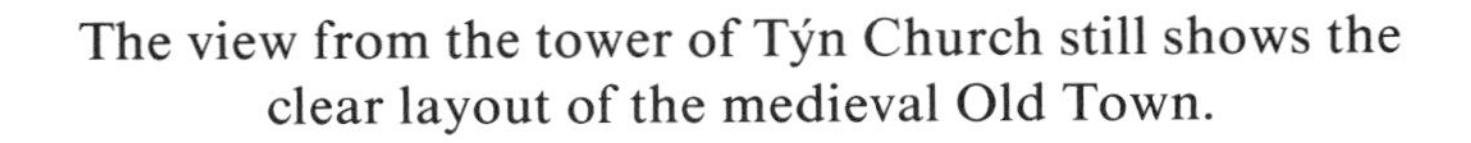
The view from the tower of Týn Church still shows the clear layout of the medieval Old Town.

The tower of the Old Town Hall from the second half of the 14th century with the oriel chapel (before 1381) and the Old Town Astronomical Clock (1410)

ly, in c. 1360 he extended the Lesser Town in a southerly direction and had it enclosed with a stone wall. Thus Prague became the largest and the most impressive town in Central Europe.

Charles IV was closely acquainted with the two leading centres of art, France and Italy. As an intellectual and art collector of exquisite taste, he ensured from the very beginning that a high artistic standard be applied in all his ambitious construction. With no less determination did he insist on the best in sculpture, painting and craftsmanship. The Palace of Prague Castle was modelled after the pattern of royal residences in Paris. He summoned a French architect Mathieu d'Arras to build his cathedral. D'Arras constructed the eight chapels of the choir ambitory with arcades. On the death of d'Arras, Charles brought in a young genius, the architect Peter Parler of Gmünd, who completed the choir, built the Golden Gate and the lower section of the adjacent tower.

Parler's masonic lodge took part in the construction of important churches in the Lesser Town (the hall of the Maltese church) and in the Old Town (Our Lady-before-Týn). At the same time other anonymous architects were busy in Prague working on many new churches and monasteries in the New Town and on Gothic houses in the other two Prague Towns. On some of them we can still admire the intricate stonework, e.g. the oriel windows of the Old Town Hall and the Carolinum. Parler's masonic lodge included leading sculptors. Peter Parler himself was architect and sculptor of the cathedral and the Old Town Bridge Tower, and also of the admirable northern portal of Týn Church (now exhibited in the National Gallery in St George's Convent)

The oriel window of the Carolinum, c. 1370, is the best preserved part of the original Gothic patrician's house, which Wenceslas IV donated to the university college in 1383.

▶

Charles Bridge, founded by Charles IV in 1357 on the site of a destroyed Romanesque bridge, Judith Bridge. The builder was Johann Ottl under the supervision of Peter Parler. The Baroque sculptures on the pillars were partly replaced by statues in the middle of the 19th century and by modern copies.

The Old Town Bridge Tower — the most beautiful Gothic gateway in Central Europe — was built by the Parler masonic lodge in the years 1380—1400. It was renovated by Josef Mocker in 1874—1878 and has recently been restored.

Emperor Charles IV on the Old Town Bridge Tower, end of 14th century

Wenceslas IV as King of Rome on the Old Town Bridge Tower, end of 14th century

and the solemn yet charming sculpture of the Virgin of the Old Town Hall (now in the Museum of the City of Prague).

At the Court of Prague there was also an active School of Painting, and in a surprisingly short time the artists there responded to French and Italian stimuli by developing a Bohemian style of Gothic painting, which reached world level in the works of the leading painters. There were also the jewellers, the goldsmiths, the carvers, the glass-makers, the metal-casters and metal-workers, the embroiderers and the producers of richly adorned cloth, some of whose best work can be seen in the Treasury of St Vitus' Cathedral and in Aachen indicating the wide range and high standard of art and craftsmanship in Prague under Charles.

Charles' character combined in a unique way the mystic piety of a medieval man, the humanist education of the new era with the restrained realism of a statesman and the cool self-interest of an economist. He was the first great collector in Bohemia, with a taste for relics as well as jewels and works of art. He made Prague a great centre of court art to enhance both the prestige of the country and of its ruler. Prague Castle was built by him not only as a comfortable home for the royal family, but as an official residence and a symbol of the state of Bohemia. During Charles' reign Prague truly became "golden", for the lead roofs of the Castle gateways shone far afield with their gilding. Something of the festive atmosphere of those days can be felt to this day in the ground floor of the present palace below Vladislav Hall, where the rooms rebuilt by Charles have largely survived.

The most conspicuous memorial of the "Father of the Country" — as Charles IV used to be called—is, of course, St Vitus' Cathedral. Although only the choir with the

The cloister of the former Emmaus
Monastery, built c. 1360. The monastery was
founded by Charles IV in 1347 to support
the Slavonic liturgy. Now the Institute of
History of the Academy of Sciences

Mural paintings in Emmaus Monastery from 1358—1362. These are some of the most valuable examples of Gothic painting at the time of Charles IV.

southern transept and the tower were built according to the original plans (the western nave and aisles and the two spires were added as late as 1873—1929) this church ranks among the best examples of Gothic architecture anywhere.

Peter Parler was an innovator of great talent, who boldly implemented his original ideas in anticipation of the Late Gothic style. The polygonal chapels built by Mathieu d'Arras were changed into square ones. Parler enlarged St Wenceslas' Chapel and made it into a separate area beyond the framework of the choir. In unique style he designed the main portico, transept and great tower. But even more importantly he applied in St Vitus' the principles and elements of Late Gothic architecture, in a manner unmatched anywhere at that time: net vaulting (in the coir and sacristy) and star vaulting (St Vitus' Chapel, sacristy), suspended keystones (sacristy), horizontal trends as compared with Gothic verticality, flamboyant motifs in the window traceries and an open spiral stairway to the external structure. Peter Parler took the net and star vaulting together with the element of flamboyant tracery from English architecture. But the complex external system of flying buttresses and the finials, the motif of the open twist and the particularly effective use of contrast — the solid arcades in the shade and the light glasshouse-like construction above the triforium filled with light —were original creations of his inventive genius.

Capital of a console of the northern portal
of Týn Church, the work of the Parler
masonic lodge, c. 1390

No less important and unusual are the sculptural decorations of the cathedral, in whose planning the Emperor himself participated. The ground floor was set aside for the past history of the Přemyslids: statue of St Wenceslas in the Saint's Chapel (1373); six tombs of Přemyslid rulers in the ambitorium chapels; the triforium presented the Luxemburg dynasty; twenty-one portrait busts of the Emperor and his family — Prague archbishops, the Master of Works and the two architects, while the upper triforium on the outside of the cathedral was consecrated to the heavenly protectors of the Kingdom and dynasty; ten relief busts of Christ, the Virgin Mary, and the patron saints of Bohemia. The extensive sculptural decorations were the work of numerous stonemasons, headed by Peter Parler, and records show that the tomb of Přemysl I was made by Parler himself.

The concept of the lower portrait gallery in the triforium, where alongside members of the reigning dynasty there were found even commoners, went beyond medieval propriety and suggests the Renaissance cult of individualism. Many busts were indeed realistic portraits. The busts of saints in the upper triforium were modelled on outstanding persons of the time. Prague sculpture stood at the van of the European development of art in its aim to portray the true likeness of a person and capture his or her character and personal qualities.

The mystical spirit of Charles' Prague can be seen most strikingly in St Wenceslas' Chapel, built around the tomb of the first Bohemian martyr. The chapel is adorned with polished semi-precious stones set in a gold plaster. Gothic mural paintings of the Passion run along the lower strip with figures of the Emperor and Empress on the altar wall; the magnificent Gothic statue of St Wenceslas with original colouring and the stonemason's mark of Peter Parler stands on the altar. The upper mural painting from the Renaissance period relates the St Wenceslas legend. The chapel has a unique and enthralling atmosphere with echoes of the Byzantine tradition. Charles IV, who deliberately encouraged the cult of St Wenceslas — the Coronation Jewels and Prague University were consecrated to St Wenceslas — seemed to want to preserve the eastern element in the Bohemian Christian tradition, which was very much alive at the time of St Wenceslas.

The tower on the façade of the Church of Our Lady-below-the-Chain, part of the Monastery of the Knights of Malta, built by the Parler masonic lodge at the end of the 14th century. Its solidity symbolizes the militant character of the Order.

Charles' admirable generosity and foresight found expression especially during the foundation and construction of the New Town of Prague. Its very location was a happy one. It adjoined the Old Town on all sides in such a manner that its main square —today's Wenceslas Square — prolonged the transverse axis of the Gall Town. Wenceslas Square also formed the bar of a cross whose upright arm led to the Haycarting Square (today's Gorky Square — náměstí Gorkého) in the lower section and to the Cattle Market (today's Charles Square — Karlovo náměstí) in the upper part of the New Town. On this basic cross in the town plan of the New Town the network of streets linked up in a functional and logical manner, and most of its layout from the period of Charles IV has survived up to the present day as it still fulfils its function. Charles IV established exceptionally favourable conditions for the rapid growth of the

Master of the Třeboň Altarpiece, St Catherine, detail of a panel of the altar in Třeboň, c. 1380. The charming, gentle and emotionally effective expression was a harbinger of the Beautiful Style. National Gallery, Prague

Circle of the Master of the Madonna of Krumlov, the Krumlov Madonna, lindentree wood, c. 1400. National Gallery, Prague

The St Vitus Madonna with the original carved frame
from the end of the 14th century represents
a culminating work of the Beautiful Style in Bohemian
Gothic panel painting. National Gallery, Prague

[63

newly founded town and its prosperity. He purchased land, forbade land speculation, laid down a rule that building construction was to start within one month and was to be completed within a year and a half, and he exempted the new inhabitants from taxes for twelve years. The New Town was given exceptionally broad and straight streets and vast squares, the dominating points of the town were enhanced by church architecture (St Catherine's at the highest point in the upper part, St Apollinarius' at Větrov, Karlov Monastery above the Nusle Valley, and Emmaus Monastery above the Vltava).

The passion for collecting seems to have inspired the Emperor to assemble in the New Town the most varied layouts in plan and vertical appearance of churches, from single naved to basilicas, churches with equal sized naves to circular ones. The need for representation as the capital city of the Empire forced Charles IV to invite monas-

Bethlehem Chapel, reconstructed by the architect Jaroslav Frágner in the years 1950—1953 on the patterns of the original chapel built in 1391 for services to be held in the Czech language and demolished in 1786. Master Jan Hus preached his sermons here in 1402—1414.

The reconstructed interior of Bethlehem Chapel, detail
of the pulpit and the door

tic Orders from distant countries of Europe to Prague (the Ambrosian Benedictines at St Ambrose's came from Milan, the Augustinians at Karlov from France, the Servites at Our Lady-of-the-Lawn "Na slupi" from Florence, and the Slavonic Benedictines at Emmaus were summoned from Croatia).

None of the many remarkable churches in the New Town has survived in its original state. The Emmaus Monastery Church of Our Lady (kostel Panny Marie Na Slovanech), which Charles built for the Slavonic Benedictines with the grand intention of putting an end to the conflict between the western and eastern churches, was destroyed by bombing on 14th February 1945 and was re-built after the war. The modern façade was designed by František M. Černý and dates from 1967. Only in the cloisters of the adjacent monastery was it possible to save part of the valuable mural paintings from the sixties of the 14th century, which represent thesis and antitheses, the confrontation of one scene of the New Testament with two analogical themes in the Old Testament. These murals are some of the most important monuments of Bohemian Gothic painting, showing an original synthesis of French and Italian stimuli.

Only the torso remains of the second Monastery Church of Our Lady-of-the-Snows (Panny Marie Sněžné) built for the Order of the Carmelites from Saxony. According to the Emperor's wishes this was to be the longest and highest church in Prague and the highest — after St Vitus' — it has remained even though its vaulting was lowered in the 17th century. If it had been completed, it would undoubtedly have been a rarity in European architecture. In its present state of Late Renaissance adaptation, the interior of the church gives a very clear idea, by its loftiness and verticality, of the sublimity of spiritual life in Gothic Prague.

Counsellors Partaking in the Utraquist Holy Communion, miniature in the *Jena Codex,* the work of illuminator Janíček Zmilelý of Písek in the early 16th century. Library of the National Museum, Prague

One important church of the Caroline period retains no more than its general layout, a hectagonal ground plan and its outside walls. This is the Church of Our Lady and Charlemagne (Panny Marie a Karla Velikého) at Karlov, inspired by Charlemagne's Chapel in Aachen. The much admired star vaulting in the nave, adapted in the Baroque period, dates from 1575. It inspired a romantic legend claiming that the architect sold his soul to the devil to ensure successful completion of his plan.

Caroline Prague also surprises and pleases with charming miniature, intimate, perfectly balanced architecture. Such an intimate little structure — vaulted on a central pillar — is the small Church of Our Lady-of-the-Lawn (Panny Marie Na trávníčku, Na slupi), lying on the old Vyšehrad road that linked the two castles of Prague. The Vyšehrad chapter church, renewed and decorated by Charles with outstanding magnificence, was completely destroyed together with the royal palace and other buildings during the Hussite Wars.

Prague under King Wenceslas IV

Gothic art reached its culmination and came to a sudden end in Prague during the reign of Charles' son Wenceslas IV (1378—1419). The son was the very opposite to his father. Neurotic, hysterical, lacking will power, he was a man that, in the end, neglected even his duties as ruler and merely followed his own interests, hunting, art collecting and court entertainment. He resided at the Royal Court in the Old Town, which used to stand where the Municipal House of the City of Prague stands today. He chose his favourites from among the lower gentry and the burghers. Thus he incurred the enmity of the Bohemian noblemen, who imprisoned him in 1394, and interference in Bohemian affairs from his brother Sigismund, King of Hungary.

In contrast to Charles, Wenceslas ran into conflict also with the higher Church hierarchy. In 1393 he even had the Archbishop's vicar, John of Pomuk, tortured and

The original Romanesque Church of St Martin-in-the-Wall, which derived its name from the town wall adjacent to it since the 13th century. It was re-built in the 14th and the 15th century. Here, in 1419, Holy Communion was celebrated in the Utraquist manner for the very first time.

The Burning of Master Jan Hus at the Stake,
the Litoměřice Gradual, before 1517.
District Museum, Litoměřice

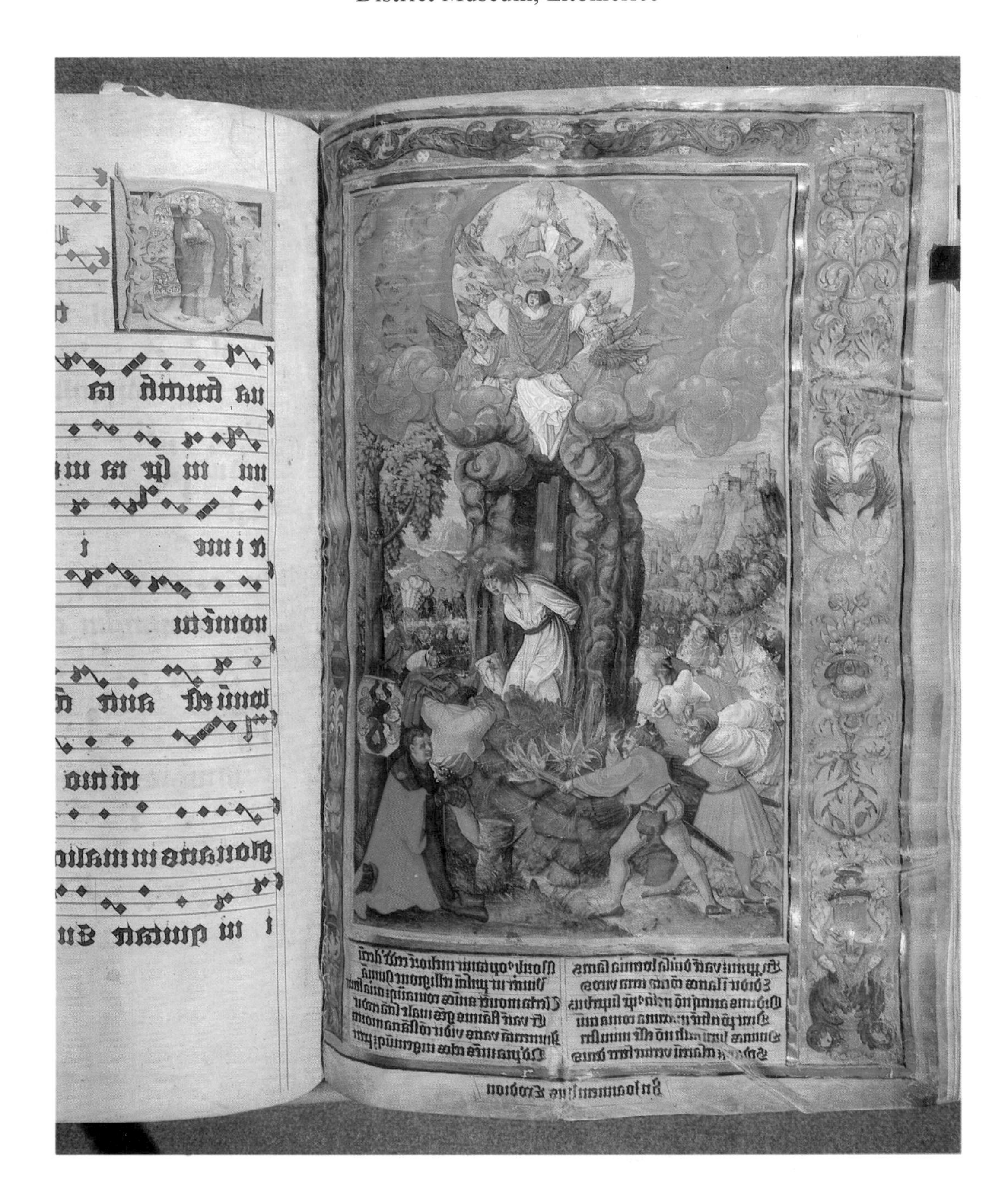

thrown into the Vltava. John of Pomuk later became a saint and was called St John of Nepomuk. In 1400 the clerical Electors removed Wenceslas IV from the throne of the King of Rome and elected Ruprecht of the Palatinate in his place.

During the weak reign of Wenceslas IV a rapid decline of the moral standards of the clergy set in, which accelerated in proportion to the power and wealth of the Church. Efforts at reform grew more intense after the papal schism in 1378, when one Pope resided in Rome and the second in Avignon, and they placed each other in ban. During the reign of Charles IV several reformers preached the necessity of moral reform in Prague and spoke out against the greed and malpractices of the clergy. Apart from the German Konrad Waldhauser, whom the Emperor summoned from Vienna, there was Jan Milíč of Kroměříž, a wandering ascetic and spellbinding preacher of the evils of the Anti-Christ. Under Wenceslas Magister Matthew of Genoa, a student from Paris, became famous, as well as Squire Tomáš of Štítný, a brilliant graduate of Prague

University, who as a layman was the first to write on religious subjects in Czech, and Magister Jeremy of Prague, who around 1400 brought from Oxford copies of John Wycliff's two main works. The most important of the Czech reformers was Jan Hus.

During the reign of Wenceslas IV building activity continued equally as swiftly as under Charles until 1400 when Prague ceased to be the residence of the King of Rome. Most unfinished buildings were completed as planned, and work continued on the con-

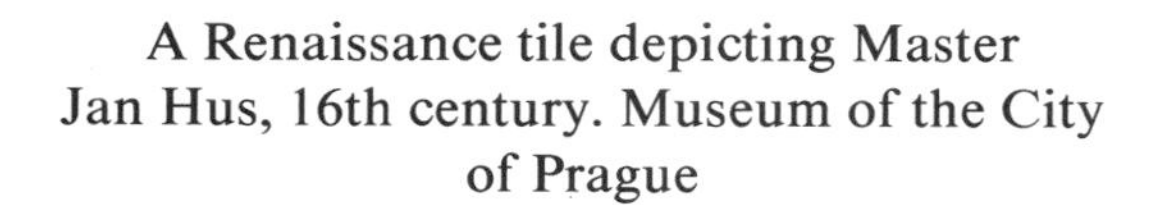

A Renaissance tile depicting Master Jan Hus, 16th century. Museum of the City of Prague

struction of Pague Castle, St Vitus' Cathedral and Týn Church on the Old Town Square. But in many of the new buildings there was a shift from the imposing monumentality of Charles' architecture towards smaller scale, sophistication in design and greater use of decorative ornamentation. A magnificent example is the hall of columns on the present-day ground floor of the Old Castle Palace, whose asymmetrical rib vaulting shows a high degree of originality.

An artistic jewel of Prague of that period is the Old Town Bridge Tower with its outstanding sculptural ornamentation. This "most beautiful of gatehouses of Central Europe" — as it has been called — perfectly combined the function of defence, representation (statues of Emperor Charles IV and King Wenceslas IV enthroned and the patron saint of Bohemia) and a symbolic function expressed in the form of a triumphal arch.

A traveller who passed through Prague in 1399 described with surprise that he had never seen so many people, a town so rich and affluent with goods. He noticed that its inhabitants had stoves instead of fireplaces and drank beer instead of wine. On Saturdays they all took a bath, men and women jointly, and they showed no embarrassment at their nakedness. He admired also the magnificent Prague churches and the royal palace adorned with the most beautiful works of art.

Painting was greatly appreciated in the atmosphere of spiritual revival during the reign of Wenceslas IV. Mural painting was no longer as much in demand as it had been during the reign of Charles, and artists now turned to panel painting and book illustrations. Instead of monumental and representative art aiming at realism and inspired by the Italian art of the sixties and partly the seventies of the 14th century (The Master of the Emmaus Cycle, Master Oswald, Master Theodoric), there was now a renewed trend towards Gothic idealism and mystical spiritualism. During the last few

The Church of Our Lady-of-the-Snows, founded by Charles IV in 1347 in memory of his coronation as King of Bohemia. It was re-built after 1606 and given the vaulting it has to this day. Only the choir was completed of the original grandiose plan. In this church Jan Želivský, the main representative of the Prague popular wing of the Hussite Revolutionary Movement, was preacher.

The New Town Hall. Built in 1377—1398, its tower dates from the middle of the 15th century, the façade was re-built in Renaissance style c. 1520. Here, on 30 July 1419, the Hussite Revolution began with the first Prague defenestration.

decades of the 14th century the people of Prague showed preference for small, intimate art forms, which were intended for spiritual contemplation or aesthetic enjoyment.

In the Collection of Gothic Art of the National Gallery in Prague — in St George's Convent at Prague Castle — we can admire the work of the Master of the Třeboň Altarpiece, the main representative of Bohemian painting in the eighties of the 14th century, who, most convincingly and at a high level of artistic quality, expressed the aspirations and emotions of his time. In the work of the Master of the Třeboň Altarpiece there culminated, in content and form, the development of Bohemian painting of the Luxemburg period. He gave a new conception to the subjects of Christian mysticism by perfectly expressing a deep personal experience of religious ideas. The ardent emotional content attains great intensity where his pictures depict and stimulate mystical experience. With artistic perfection he embodied the ideas of the onsetting movement of *devotio moderna*, supported by the Luxemburg and members of the lead-

ing Church hierarchy and spread in particular by the Augustinian Order. The Master of the Třeboň Altarpiece, a leading personality among 14th century European painters, created a unique synthesis of existing Bohemian painting and progressive Franco-Flemish currents. Through his personal contribution, an attempt at chiaroscuro, he greatly influenced both the Beautiful Style of around 1400 and the whole of Central European painting far into the first half of the 15th century.

The Prague of Wenceslas IV became a place where the Beautiful Style was born, found ideal conditions for its development and left a mark on the art of other European countries. The Beautiful Style was characteristic of feudal society at the time of its decline. At a period when social contradictions grew sharper, the upper strata of feudal society withdrew into isolation and formed secret societies with intricate ceremonials, symbols and badges. They surrounded themselves with luxury and the showy ostentation of Court life, indulged in fads and amusements, in brief, they tried in every possible manner to escape unpleasant reality by seeking refuge in fanciful idealism.

Art at that time was primarily concerned with aesthetics, and it turned away from reality towards Mannerism. But it did not avoid realistic elements; on the contrary, it made use of sophisticated contrast, abstract composition and decorative draperies. The most beautiful example of this style is the St Vitus Madonna (in the National Gallery in Prague). The rare harmony of all its parts and perfect technical execution makes it

◀
The larger Late Gothic Lesser Town Bridge Tower was built in 1464, probably on the site of an older Romanesque tower of Judith Bridge, which will have stood here together with the lower Romanesque tower. The gateway between the two towers was fashioned during the reign of Wenceslas IV after 1411.

Hussite shield in the Old Town coat-of-arms from the 15th century. Museum of the City of Prague

Late Gothic stone pulpit in Týn Church, with paintings by Josef Hellich of 1874

Gothic christening font of pewter, 1414, from the Church of Our Lady-before-Týn

a classical work of the Beautiful Style at its height. It is assumed that it came from the workshop of the Master of the Krumlov Madonna, who together with the Master of the Torun Madonna, stood as an artist in the forefront of the application of the Beautiful Style in sculpture. It should be mentioned that the Beautiful Style grew out of the traditions of Peter Parler's masonic lodge, and that these two masters have hypothetically been identified as his successors.

We can look at least at a replica of the Krumlov Madonna in the National Gallery in Prague — the original belongs to the Kunsthistorisches Museum in Vienna — but not a single volume of the extensive library of Wenceslas IV remained in Prague. And it is in these manuscripts (now in the National Library in Vienna) illuminated with exquisite taste and witty inventiveness that we can find a good deal about social life at Wenceslas' Court in Prague and the spiritual life in the town just before the Hussite Revolution. The manuscripts in many places contain the motif of a kingfisher in a wreath, a bathwoman or a man in the stocks as symbols of the relationship of love between King and Queen.

Hussite Prague

The Hussite Revolution was the first reform and anti-feudal movement in Europe. It had long been developing, and the reign of Charles IV unwillingly contributed most to its outbreak.

This was due to the rapidly growing power of the Church, based on immense possession, which inevitably roused opposition, particularly when corruption increased with the growing wealth of the Church, and the life of the priests and monks became steadily more dissipated. Roughly one half of all farmsteads in the country belonged to the Church. In the twenty-five monasteries, which stood in Prague at the end of the 14th century, there lived at least 500 monks and nuns, many in a profligate manner. Opposition to them was growing among the people of Prague particularly when the town's prosperity declined and difficulties set in.

Apart from monks there was the clergy, the prelates of the five Chapters of the Archbishopric, priests, chaplains and a countless number of clergymen of varying status, each hoping to assume some Church office. These offices were for sale, and the most important and most profitable were distributed by the Papal See in return for bribes. Enmity against the Church grew since most of the heavy town rates were collected by the Church institutions, which were of a distinct usurious character, and these institutions had no qualms in carrying out financial transaction at the expense of the town's people.

The power and wealth of the Church was nothing out of the ordinary at that time, but in Prague it came to assume an exceptional scale. The expansion of the town began to stagnate when it ceased to be a residence of the King of Rome, and in consequence

◀ The façade of the Church of Our Lady-before-Týn on the Old Town Square. Gothic nave and aisles from the second half of the 14th century. The second most important church in Prague after St Vitus' Cathedral. A statue of King George of Poděbrady stood in the Late Gothic gable after 1463 together with a gilded chalice. It was replaced by a gilded statue of the Virgin in 1626. The northern tower, built in the years 1463—1466, was newly built after a fire in 1835. The southern tower was finished in 1511. In front of the church stands the Gothic Týn School with a Renaissance gable, where architect Matěj Rejsek was headmaster.

there was a drop in production. It was then that the conflicts between the rich patriciate and the town craftsmen and hired labourers led to a social crisis. The time for revolution was ripe, and all that was needed was a leader. He was found in Master Jan Hus of Charles University.

Hus had gained popularity as a preacher in Bethlehem Chapel (Betlémská kaple), which was founded in 1391 by two Prague citizens as a place where sermons were to be preached in Czech. Here Hus began to preach in 1402 in support of Wycliff's teaching, which before long divided the masters of Prague University into two sharply opposing camps. Hus' greatness rests in his managing to link the local movement of *devotio moderna* and the progressive Western ideology of the time and in giving expression to the people's opposition to the parasitic character of the Church and the social injustice of feudal society. All classes of Prague citizens gathered to hear Hus' ser-

The southern façade of the Old Town Hall. Its core is formed by the house of merchant Kříž purchased by the community in the middle of the 14th century. The Renaissance window here dates from 1520—1528. In 1458 the adjacent house of furrier Mikeš was added to this, its Neo-Renaissance front dates from 1880. The Empire House "At the Cock" was bought up in 1830.

mons in Bethlehem Chapel, in particular small craftsmen and apprentices, but the audience included even Queen Sophie. And Hus seemed to speak to everybody's mind when in the way of all reformers he turned to the Gospels and contrasted the original Church of Christ with the contemporary corrupt Church of Rome.

Bethlehem Chapel, one of the most sacred works of architecture of the Czech nation, was re-built in 1950—1952 in its original form by the architect Josef Frágner and was adorned on the walls with pictures taken from the *Jena Codex* in which there survives the Hussite antithesis sharply criticizing the Catholic Church.

Hus' supporters won their first great success in 1409 when on the Master's proposal Wenceslas IV proclaimed the Kutná Hora Decree giving the Czechs at Prague University three votes and all other nationalities one vote. This changed the ratio of the votes as laid down by the founder of the University, Charles IV. The matter came to a head with the convening of the Church Council, which was to settle the problem of the two Popes, where the Germans opposed the King. The German masters and students in protest against this Decree left Prague and moved to Leipzig, and Jan Hus became the Rector of the now entirely Czech university.

As long as the King backed Hus the enmity of the Church leaders was not dangerous for him. The Archbishop's ban imposed for his failure to enforce the papal prohibition of preaching in private chapels had no effect. But when in 1412 Hus parted ways with the King over the matter of selling indulgences — Wenceslas had permitted their sale

The Old Council Chamber in the Old Town Hall from the third quarter of the 15th century with the original coats-of-arms of the Prague guilds on the walls

The Man of Sorrows, Late Gothic statue from the first half of the 15th century in the Old Council Chamber in the Old Town Hall

in return for a commission, events began to take a rapid turn. Hus voluntarily left Prague to live in the countryside. In 1414 he went, also voluntarily, to the Council of Constance to defend his views. But the Council would not admit any free discussion, in which the main criterion was the Holy Scripture. No one refuted Hus' arguments and views, hence Hus refused to withdraw his teaching, and was burnt at the stake on 6 July 1415.

550 years later the Catholic Church at the Second Vatican Council revised the verdict and rehabilitated Jan Hus. At the time, however, this transgression of justice resulted in a phenomenon that the prelates of the Council of Constance had been trying to avoid. The Czech nation backed by their gentry stood up for Hus in opposition to the Council. They regarded Hus as martyr of the true faith, and his degrading death an insult to the entire nation. The people began to confiscate Church lands, destroy monasteries and expel the monks, who refused to take the Utraquist (i.e. the host and the wine). This novelty — inspired by the Gospel — was introduced by Master Jakoubek of Stříbro, Hus' successor in Bethlehem Chapel, and before his death it had been approved by Hus in Constance. The chalice with the wine became, for a long time to come, the symbol of supporters of Jan Hus.

Wenceslas IV, under pressure from his brother Sigismund, tried to prevent the anti-Church uprisings, but he met with resistance. When the people of the New Town under the leadership of Jan Želivský, the preacher at the Church of Our Lady-of-the-Snows, threw counsellors and burghers out of the windows of the New Town Hall on 30 July 1419, Wenceslas IV suffered a stroke as a result of the event and died on 16 August. His brother Sigismund as King of Hungary and Roman Emperor laid claim to the Bohemian throne but refused to rule over a heretic nation and decided to enforce the Catholic faith by force. A crusade was proclaimed against the Hussite Czechs, and Prague saw itself forced to organize its military defence. For it was still true that whoever ruled over Prague ruled over Bohemia.

The ideological basis for the unified platform of various Hussite parties were the Four Prague Articles, demanding freedom of preaching, the Utraquist communion, the denial of secular power to priests, and the punishment of deadly sins. The people of Prague agreed on this programme with another revolutionary group who came to their aid from Tábor under the leadership of Jan Žižka of Trocnov. His foresightedness helped to repel the Crucaders' attack on Vítkov Hill on 14 July 1420, and the Hussites celebrated their first victory over the numerically far stronger and better equipped enemy. And when Sigismund's army attacked a second time in vain below

The Late Gothic portal of the Old Town Hall

80]

The Old Town Astronomical Clock, the work of Mikuláš of Kadaň (c. 1410), perfected by Master Hanuš in c. 1490. The sculptural ornaments date from the beginning and the end of the 15th century, the Apostles were made by Vojtěch Sucharda in 1948. The panel with the calendar is a copy of the original by Josef Mánes of 1866.

[81

The oldest view of Prague of the year 1493, a woodcut
by Michael Wohlgemut and Wilhelm Pleydenwurff
in Hartmann Schedel's book *Liber cronicarum*

Vyšehrad on 1 November 1420, the Hussite soldiers gradually acquired the aura of invincibility. This was enhanced at every further victory over the Crusaders' army. A total of five times the Crusaders fought the Hussites, but always in vain. The last campaign was attended by the Papal Legate Cardinal Cesarini, who found out for himself that the best thing to do was to turn tail on the Hussites and run.

From the beginning of the Hussite Revolution Prague played a leading role, but the people were never united in their opinions. The Old Town folk held more conservative views, the new Town citizens were radical, which corresponded to the social and ethnic structure of the two towns. The third — the Lesser Town — was so completely destroyed in November 1419 before the battle of Vítkov that it, in fact, ceased to exist. The political importance of Prague rose fast at the very beginning of the Revolution when, in the spring of 1421, it assumed the leadership of a union of royal towns. In June that year, its representatives, for the first time, sat in the leading position at the Land Diet at Čáslav. This important Diet rejected Sigismund's claim to the throne of Bohemia and instead of a king elected twenty governors to administer the country. Among these were eight burghers, and of these four were men from Prague.

To increase their political weight the people of the Old and of the New Town extended their military union into a joint administration. But the conflicts between them did not disappear, and the link-up lasted for no more than two and a half years.

The conflict of interests between the burghers, who wanted a return to stability and prosperity, and the town poor, who had reaped no benefits from the Revolution, was brought to a head by their spokesman Jan Želivský. In October 1421 he established a short-lived revolutionary dictatorship. The Old Town counsellors had Želivský arrested and executed without a proper trial on 9 March 1422 in the courtyard of the Old Town Hall. From then on the people of Prague supported the moderate wing of the Hussite movement until the end. They were even in favour of seeking compromise with the Church by diplomatic negotiation.

After the failure of the last crusade the Church had come to the conclusion that Bohemia could not be defeated by military means. When the compromise, known as the Basle Compact, was reached, it meant the acknowledgement by the Council of Basle of the Four Prague Articles though in limited form. Whereupon the Church enlisted the help of the Bohemian nobility to deal with the radical Hussites at the battle of Lipany in 1431. The hitherto unbeatable Hussite army under Jan Žižka's outstanding successor Prokop Holý was defeated here by an alliance of moderate Prague people and the catholic gentry.

This opened the way for Emperor Sigismund to become King of Bohemia. Before this could happen Sigismund had to issue a Charter to the people of Prague, in which he confirmed their permanent ownership of the property confiscated from the Church. He also agreed that none of the emigrants would be allowed to return or to have confiscated property restored to them and that only Czechs and Utraquists should hold town offices.

When other benefits that the Hussite Revolution brought to Prague are added, such as the nullification of any financial claims by the Church and, in particular, of mortgages on houses, it becomes clear that Prague burghers gained benefits they had not even dreamt of before the Revolution. For that reason the citizens of Prague watched in embarrassed silence when Sigismund had Žižka's fellow-leader and the last

The town coat-of-arms of the Old Town in the Royal Charter of King Vladislav II of Jagiello of the year 1477. Archives of the City of Prague

Commander of Tábor Jan Roháč of Dubá executed on the Old Town Square in 1437 together with sixty-five of his companions, who regarded the agreement with Sigismund as a betrayal of the Hussite ideals.

The Hussite Revolution and the long years of war caused immense damage. One third of Bohemia was laid waste, the population was on the decline, the economy run down, agriculture upset. There were particularly unfavourable consequences in international trade, from which the country was excluded and its role taken over by Leipzig.

The Powder Tower, the main work of Matěj Rejsek in Prague, from the years 1475—1489. Reconstructed in 1875—1886 by the architect Josef Mocker, renovated in 1962—1963. The most ornamental work of Prague Late Gothic formed a dignified entrance to the Old Town.

84]

Late Gothic baldaquin by Matěj Rejsek,
1493, in the Church of Our Lady-before-Týn,
made for the tomb of Bishop Augustin
Lucian of Mirandola

Art, too, suffered heavy and irreplaceable losses. The building of churches was interrupted — St Vitus' remained unfinished until the 19th century — and the artists left Prague. A multitude of works of architecture, sculpture, painting and craftmanship were destroyed. The convents and monasteries suffered most. The Hussites spared only Emmaus and the Monastery of the Knights of the Cross, since both joined the uprising in time. Numerous sculptures and panel painting vanished from the churches, chalices and monstrances were turned into coins. This iconoclasm did not give rise to the Old Testament fears of idolatry. The people in their raving destroyed valuable objects for the simple reason that they had been made with the money they had surrendered in the form of various dues.

The Hussite Movement did try to create its own new art, and though there was little time and very unfavourable conditions they succeeded quite well in certain spheres. The Hussite songs became the first popular revolutionary songs in the history of world music. The Hussite Movement generally raised the importance of the Czech language

Late Gothic bell-tower by the Church of St Henry from the years 1472—1476, restored by the architect Josef Mocker in 1879

and introduced it into liturgy and divine services. Czech as a civilized language, suitable for the expression of the most complex concepts of theology and law, spread to the surrounding countries and in the second half of the 15th century was used as a diplomatic language in Central Europe. The Hussites contributed to Czech literature not only copies of the Bible, some with magnificent illuminations, but even satirical poetry. They tried to bring culture to everybody as witnessed by a statement from one of their chief opponents Aeneas Piccolomini, the future Pope Pius II: "Their perfidious human race has a sole good quality, they love education."

86]

The Late Gothic Town

Emperor Sigismund died in 1437 after a brief reign, and after the interrupted rule of his son-in-law Albrecht of Habsburg and thirteen years without a monarch, finally Albrecht's son Ladislav, called Posthumus, received the Crown of Bohemia in 1453. He was still a boy at the time, and George of Poděbrady, leader of the Utraquist Party, acted as regent. George proved himself a good administrator. Within a short time he achieved the consolidation of a country upset by wars and managed to lead it towards prosperity.

Ladislav did not live to celebrate his wedding with the French Princess Magdalene; he died suddenly at the early age of seventeen. In 1458 George of Poděbrady was elected King of Bohemia. This circumstance clearly indicates that the Hussite Revolution had raised the political importance of the towns and mainly the capital city of Prague.

Late Gothic waterworks tower, the so-called Šítek Tower, of the year 1495, renovated in 1591 and re-built after 1648, with a Baroque onion tower from the end of the 18th century. From the tower water was run through wooden pipes to the fountains of the New Town. The 15th century Šítek's mills were replaced in 1930 by the present building of the Mánes Union of Artists, designed by Otakar Novotný.

George of Poděbrady sat on the throne of Bohemia one hundred years after Emperor Charles IV. He was a strong personality, who, in the changed conditions, tried to renew once more the former power and prosperity of medieval Bohemia. George was a master at balancing conflicting forces and trends to achieve political compromise. The basis of his home and foreign policy were the Basle Compacts, which were to ensure the country the necessary peace and peaceful coexistence with Catholic Europe and the Church of Rome.

The brief period of peaceful coexistence with papacy, however, came finally to an end when Pius II was elected to the Holy See and in 1462 proclaimed the Compacts invalid. George tried to find a way out of his international political isolation by a bold plan for a League of Christian Rulers in defence against the Turks, from which the Pope was excluded. The result of his grandiose plan, far ahead of its time, were bilateral treaties with the Kings of France and of Poland.

When the Pope imposed a ban on George and proclaimed a Crusade against Bohemia, this was taken up by George's former son-in-law Matthias Corvinus, the King of Hungary, who wanted the Crown of Bohemia for himself. Until his premature death George had military and political supremacy over Matthias as he won the Kings of Rome and Poland over to his side. To prevent Matthias from being elected King of Bohemia, he did not hesitate to exclude his own sons from the succession and approved as his successor the candidature of the son of King Casimir of Poland, the young Vladislav of Jagiello.

One decade was sufficient for George to raise Bohemia to economic and cultural prosperity. He made use of the ordinary and the royal towns headed by Prague and tried

Head of St John, house sign from the first half of the 16th century. Museum of the City of Prague

as King of the Utraquists and the Catholics alike to establish a firm government of national unity, which would ensure internal peace and affluence. He did his best to stimulate foreign trade interrupted by the Hussite wars, but the Pope marred these plans. There are historical records to prove that there existed trade relations between Prague and Switzerland and perhaps even Holland.

In the period of George of Poděbrady we can find a revival of building activity and art work. The gable and the northern tower of Týn Church were completed, new fortifications were constructed, the re-building of the Lesser Town proceeded with the erection of the larger of the Bridge Towers, and work began on the renovation of the Old Town Hall. King George well understood the importance of art for the prestige of the state. It is a pity that the equestrian statue of the King on Charles Bridge has not survived nor his statue with a drawn sword, which once stood below the large, gilded Chalice at the top of the chief Utraquist Church of Our Lady-before-Týn. The statue and the chalice were removed after the Battle of the White Mountain together with

Statue of St Wenceslas, first half of the 16th century, from the Romanesque Church of St Wenceslas at Prosek. Museum of the City of Prague

[89

The Late Gothic royal oratory in St Vitus' Cathedral (1493) with the coats-of-arms of the countries of Vladislav of Jagiello, the work of Hans Spyss of Frankfurt-am-Main

Late Gothic silver reliquary bust
of St Wenceslas in the St Vitus Treasure, last
quarter of 15th century

the motto "Truth Prevails", which was incorporated after the First World War into the coat-of-arms of Czechoslovakia.

The coronation of Vladislav of Jagiello in August 1471 brought the Polish royal family to the throne of Bohemia, and for half a century their reign represented the culmination of the age-old endeavours of the Bohemian nobility to have the country run by the Estates. The fifteen-year old Vladislav came to the throne at a time when the situation at home and abroad was difficult, since part of the Bohemian nobility acknowledged Matthias Corvinus as King of Bohemia. Constant wars laid the country waste, and Bohemia was isolated from Moravia and the other lands of the Bohemian Crown, where Corvinus ruled. Under these circumstances the demands of the nobility increased in their endeavour to dominate both the King and the towns. To raise their incomes they began to engage in economic activity with ruthless disregard for the ancient privileges of the towns.

The reputation Vladislav had as a weak monarch, easily dominated by the nobility, probably explains why after the death of Corvinus he was elected King of Hungary in 1490. For Bohemia this meant that the Hungarian Crown was once again united with Moravia and the neighbouring countries as a state of Bohemia without financial claims, and this led to the further intensification of the rule of the Estates, for the King had settled permanently in Hungarian Budín and paid only rare visits to Prague.

Vladislav Hall in Prague Castle, the most monumental hall of Gothic Prague and in Central Europe. It was built by the architect Benedikt Ried in the years 1487—1502 and covered with intricate Late Gothic lierne vaulting. The northern windows of 1493 already have a Renaissance form.

The acquisition of the Crown of Hungary brought to a head the competition between the House of Habsburg and that of Jagiello. It led to a mutual compromise, and culminated in an agreement at the Congress of Vienna of 1515 to divide the spheres of influence by means of marriage arrangements. The struggle for political hegemony was decided finally at the unfortunate Battle of Mohacs in Hungary in 1526, in which Louis, the twenty-year-old King of Bohemia and Hungary, fell. He was Vladislav's only son and the last male descendant of the Bohemian branch of the Jagiello dynasty.

In the Vladislav period the authoritativeness and strictness of the Utraquist church limited progress in ideas even more than the dogmatism of the Catholic Church had done. No wonder that a new Czech Congregation arose, the Unity of Czech Brethren. They attracted all those interested in deepening religious life and in carrying out a practical programme of Christianity according to the Holy Writ.

The Unity had come into existence in the village of Kunvald in East Bohemia already during the reign of George of Poděbrady. Its founder came from the Emmaus Monastery in Prague; he was Brother Gregory, the nephew ot the Hussite Archbishop Jan Rokycana. The Czech Brethren based their ideas on the work of the South Bohemian squire Petr Chelčický, who, as a reaction to the Hussite Wars, had proclaimed passive "non-resistance to evil", opposed all manner of force, but demanded voluntary poverty and strict moral discipline. The Unity was persecuted by King George and King Vladislav, but that simply increased its popularity and encouraged the enrollment of further supporters.

Vladislav of Jagiello, like George of Poděbrady before him, resided at the Royal Court in the Old Town. In honour of Vladislav the Old Town inhabitants began to build a new city gatehouse by the side of his residence, which, from the end of the 17th century on, was called the Powder Tower (Prašná brána), after the gunpowder that was stored there. But in 1483 the town's people rebelled against the patriciate, who were

The Riders' Steps with lierne vaulting and severed ribs were made by Benedikt Ried around 1500. Knights used them to bring their horses from the courtyard to Vladislav Hall where tournaments were held.

[93

Late Gothic net vaulting in the passageway of the House "At the Little White Horse" on the Old Town Square by Matěj Rejsek (1496). In 1848 Bedřich Smetana set up a Music School here.

attempting the reintroduction of Catholicism; they occupied the town hall and beat or executed the reactionary counsellors. The King began to be afraid of living among the rebellious town's people and moved to the Castle, where he set afoot further reconstruction work.

After the preparatory period under George of Poděbrady, building activity in Prague intensified both in quality and quantity in the Jagiello era. The two town halls, in the Old and the New Towns, were re-constructed in the new Late Gothic style, certain Catholic churches were restored, burghers houses were renovated and given intricate decorations. At that time, around 1490, Master Hanuš perfected the famous astronomical clock on the Old Town Hall, made by Mikuláš of Kadaň in 1410. In the last century Josef Mánes, the founder of Czech national painting, painted the calendar panel on this astronomical clock. It was damaged during the May Uprising in Prague in 1945 and repaired after the war.

Two artists of great talent gave Prague Late Gothic architecture, known as Vladislav architecture, its characteristic local form and raised it once again to a European level.

The first was a Czech, Matěj Rejsek of Prostějov, who earned his nickname "the shrew" when he was a shrewish teacher of draughtsmanship at the Týn School on the Old Town Square. But he gave up teaching and became an assistant to Master Wenceslas, the builder of the Powder Tower. As a self-taught man, he worked in so agile a manner that within two years he took over his master's function.

Rejsek was not an artist of genius, he thought and felt in terms of space, but he was a unique decorator with an inborn gift for picturesque detail. He followed up the local Parlerian tradition which he transposed to its Late Gothic form suppressing tectonics and stressing sensual enjoyment. His most important work in Prague — the Powder Tower — had its pattern in the Old Town Bridge Tower, but in Rejsek's design the decorative features strikingly outweigh the constructive ones. The present-day appearance of the Tower dates from 1875—1886 when Josef Mocker restored the gateway.

Rejsek's decorativeness and inventive fantasy can also be appreciated on the Old Town Hall where he designed a Late Gothic portal and a window with rich decorations of

The Daliborka Tower, built by Benedikt Ried in 1492—1494 and named after Knight Dalibor of Kozojedy, the first prisoner here. It rises above the Stag Moat of Prague Castle.

The guild casket of the New Town butchers, end of 15th century. Museum of the City of Prague

carved flowers, crabs and the sculptured emblems of Prague and Bohemia. He designed another portal and net vaulting in the passageway of the House "At the White Horse" (U bílého koníčka) on the Old Town Square, where in 1848 the Czech composer Bedřich Smetana opened his Music School. In Týn Church Rejsek made the baldaquin above the Neo-Gothic altar of St Luke.

The second artist, Benedikt Ried or Rejt, was a German from Upper Austria. He was summoned to Prague and raised the Gothic art to its climax taking it to the threshold of the Renaissance. In contrast to the decorative approach of Rejsek, Ried had an inborn sense for space and embodied his architectural genius in a grandiose building which to this day is impressive for its bold construction and majestic appearance.

By lucky force of circumstance Ried was invited to be Vladislav's leading royal architect in charge of the rebuilding of Prague Castle. Thanks to him Prague once again took its place at the van of artistic development. Ried designed Vladislav Hall with intricate lierne vaulting, reconstructed the Old Diet dating from the period of Charles IV and built a new Renaissance wing, Louis Wing, of Prague Castle. Furthermore, he made the southern Renaissance portal of the Church of St George at the Castle and even drew up plans for the completion of St Vitus' Cathedral. Unfortunately, this was never carried out for lack of funds. He built the fortification of the Castle, including the Daliborka Tower, named after the first knight to be imprisoned there. The story of Dalibor of Kozojedy, who was cast into the dungeon there in 1498, was retold by Bedřich Smetana in the opera *Dalibor*.

Vladislav Hall with the mighty waves of lierne vaulting represents the dignified end of medieval Prague. Its Renaissance windows — made by Benedikt Ried in 1493 — are a harbinger of the new style in art that was about to set in and with it an entire new era.

Renaissance Intermezzo

Renaissance tile from the New Town Hall
with the emblem of the town, 16th century.
Museum of the City of Prague

The Arrival and Welcome of St Wenceslas at the Imperial Diet in Regensburg, mural painting by the Master of the Litoměřice Altarpiece in St Wenceslas' Chapel of St Vitus' Cathedral, before 1509

The Coming of the Habsburgs

The southern windows of Vladislav Hall — the Renaissance jewel on the Late Gothic body of the Royal Palace — symbolize the importance and function of Renaissance art in Prague, and the limits it never exceeded. For the Renaissance basically did not change the medieval character of the town whose layout it determined, dominating features laid down and main mass modelled in a most creative form during the reign of the Luxemburg dynasty.

The 16th century, which was the time of Renaissance art in Bohemia, did indeed enrich Prague with a number of beautiful and remarkable works of architecture. In the first place there were built palaces and summer palaces, the entire network of streets and enclosed squares with a picturesque background of broad house fronts opening on the ground floor with shady arcades, adorned with black and white sgraffito and rising to inventively shaped gables. The Gothic verticals of the town, which continued to determine its medieval character, were balanced by the Renaissance horizontals of palaces and softened by the curves of Renaissance roofs.

At core Prague remained a Gothic city below the Renaissance façade; it continued to live in gothically conceived buildings until the Baroque period.

The Jagiello period, when the first echoes of the Italian Renaissance made themselves felt in Prague, represents only the foreword to the main chapter, which began when the Habsburgs ascended the throne of Bohemia. At that time direct contacts were established with Italy, the land of the new style, while Benedikt Rejt had been content with inspiration derived from Hungarian Budín, which thanks to Matthias Corvinus and his Italian orientation was far ahead of Prague at that time.

The Habsburgs had long striven to rule over the Kingdom of Bohemia, which was the key to their hegemony over Central Europe. They tried to achieve this three times, first when the Přemyslids died out in 1306, for the second time when the Luxemburg dynasty came to a close, and they were successful only at their third attempt. In 1526, after the death of Louis of Jagiello, Ferdinand I was elected King of Bohemia, and the House of Habsburgs remained on the throne of Bohemia until October 1918.

Ferdinand I did not achieve his aim without difficulties. When he referred to his marriage to Anne of Jagiello and treaties of inheritance between the Habsburgs and the Jagiello dynasty, the Bohemian Estates did not acknowledge these claims. Ferdinand found himself greatly in debt before he managed to convince the Bohemian Estates. First and foremost he had to promise to uphold their traditional political rights. Since

King Vladislav II of Jagiello and his Wife Queen Anne, mural painting by the Master of the Litoměřice Altarpiece in St Wenceslas' Chapel of St Vitus' Cathedral, before 1509

[99

The Renaissance Louis Wing of the Old Palace at Prague Castle, the work of Benedikt Ried in 1502—1510. The second Prague Defenestration was carried out from the windows on the second floor on 23 May 1618.

he simultaneously became King of Hungary — and his older brother had ceded to him the Austrian Lands — he could finally try to realize the old plan for a vast empire on the Danube, which the Přemyslids had visualized as the descendant of the Great Moravian Empire and for which Přemysl Otakar II had paid with his life. Irony of fate had it that it was the Habsburgs who spoilt the Přemyslid plans.

The political aspirations of Ferdinand I were only part of a larger plan harboured by the Habsburgs to rule the world. After an interlude of 200 years they used suitable marriages to take over extensive regions, the rich Netherlands, Burgundy, Spain, and new territories overseas. Emperor Charles V could proudly claim that the sun never set on his empire. To ensure the rule over so many countries, they leant towards absolutism, strengthened feudalism and limited the rights of the towns.

Today it might seem incomprehensible why the people in Bohemia, mainly Utraquist and supporters of the Estates, elected a German and a Catholic as their King. There were clearly two serious reasons for this at the time. They assumed that Ferdinand as Catholic would reach an understanding between Bohemia and the Church of Rome, and as Habsburg would be able to protect them the better from the threat of the Turks. Some considered Ferdinand a Latin rather than a German, since he had been educated in Spain and learnt German only at a later stage. To judge by his teacher, the famous humanist Erasmus of Rotterdam, he was expected to be a tolerant Catholic and all the more so since he was in disgrace with the Pope.

Unfortunately none of these expectations came true. There never was a reconciliation with the Catholic Church and the Pope, even though Ferdinand aimed at this. The permission to take Holy Communion in the Utraquist manner was an insignificant concession when approved by the Council of Trident in 1564 in view of the anti-Reformation programme proclaimed at this Council. The King introduced the Jesuit Or-

The Renaissance windows of Vladislav Hall, the work of the architect Benedikt Ried in 1493, the first sign of the Renaissance in Bohemian architecture

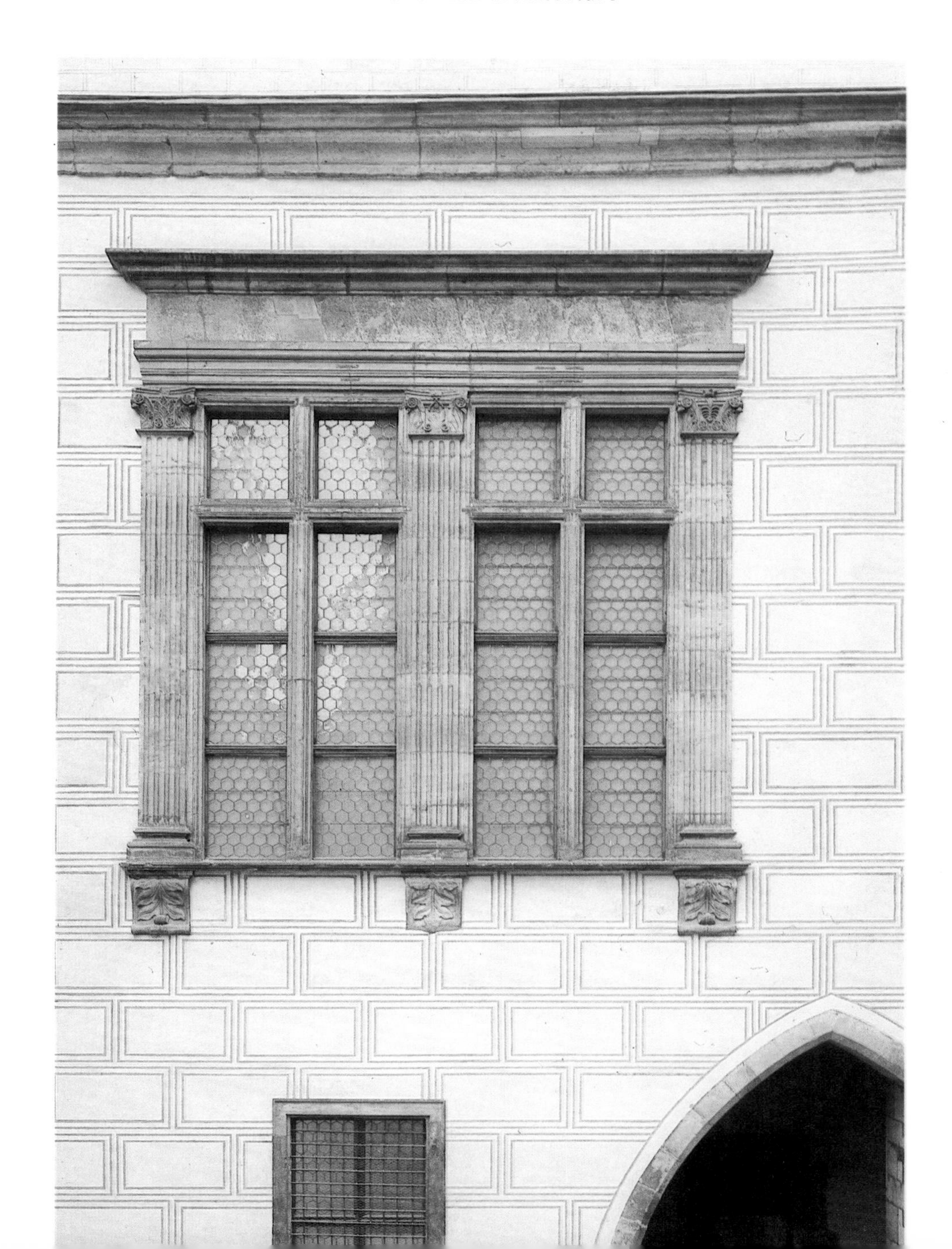

The Renaissance southern portal of St George's Basilica at Prague Castle from the early 16th century by Benedikt Ried with a Late Gothic relief of St George Fighting the Dragon. The original of this relief is now in the National Gallery.

der with its anti-Reformation programme into Bohemia, and they established their main headquarters in Prague and used it as the springboard for expansion to the East. The war against the Turks did break out, but Ferdinand only defended the western part of Hungary and Slovakia. The treasury of the state of Bohemia was the main contributor of funds for these battles. And in regard to religious tolerance, Ferdinand at first acted in restrained manner. But in 1546 he supported his brother Emperor Charles — with whom, from 1531 on, he shared the rule as King of Rome — in the war against the German Protestants. At that point the first Bohemian anti-Habsburg uprising took place headed by Prague and the royal towns, which had won over the majority of the Bohemian nobility.

The indecision of the leaders of the uprising, whose armies did not take part in the war, had tragic results. After the victorious battle of Mühlberg in 1547 Ferdinand returned to Bohemia as an angry sovereign and strictly punished the resisting Estates. Prague and the royal towns were deprived of all their land and privileges, their self-administration was restricted, two knights and burghers were executed, others imprisoned. Even though the towns soon received their privileges back, the period of political independence of the Bohemian towns had come to a definite end. The Diet acknowledged the hereditary claims of Queen Anne to the throne of Bohemia, which had been rejected in 1526 when circumstances had been different.

Since Ferdinand regarded the Unity of Bretheren as the main cause of the uprising apart from the towns, he had their meeting places closed and their members exiled from the country. In his last years, under the influence of the Council of Trident, he set his rule on a sharp course of re-Catholization and so from the middle of the 16th century insoluble religious and social contradictions grew which came to a head at the beginning of the following century and caused the Thirty Years' War.

The Old Jewish Cemetery, where burials took place from the first half of the 15th century until 1787. It contains 20,000 tombs, and the most frequently visited of these is the Renaissance tombstone of the famous Rabbi Löwe (d. 1609), the creator of the renowned Golem.

The Belvedere, the Royal Summer Palace in the Royal Garden at Prague Castle, was designed by the Italian architect Paolo della Stella in 1538—1552. The upper floor and the roof were finished by Bonifaz Wolmut in 1557—1563. One of the most beautiful Renaissance buildings outside Italy.

Ferdinand I of Habsburg Hands his Wife Anne of Jagiello a Flower, relief on the Royal Summer Palace made in the masonic lodge of Paolo della Stella, c. 1540. After this relief the building began to be called Queen Anne's Summer Palace in the 19th century.

The Renaissance Castle

Ferdinand I did not chose Prague as permanent residence and capital of the Danube Empire, but he spent a good deal of time at Prague Castle and began to extend it. By filling in the moat in front of the western gateways there arose what is today the second courtyard of the Castle. On its northern side the King had a Renaissance horse-stable built, and a Renaissance gallery with an onion tower was erected on the great tower of the cathedral.

Far more important was the layout of the Royal Garden on the northern side of the Castle and its building up in Renaissance architectural style. One of the first gardens in the Italian style north of the Alps was laid out on Ferdinand's wishes by the gardener Francesco in 1534.

In the Royal Garden stands one of the most beautiful Renaissance buildings north of Italy, the Royal Summer Palace, the Belvedere. Since a relief at one end depicts Ferdinand I handing flowers to his queen, it has become known romantically as the Summer Palace of Queen Anne. The model and design of the building was the work of an Italian architect and stonemason, Paolo della Stella, who worked here in 1535—1537, and all the reliefs were produced in his workshop. Construction began in 1538, and after a fire in 1541 rebuilding took place until 1563 when the Court Architect Bonifaz

Renaissance window on the southern front of the Old Town Hall from 1520—1528, with the golden inscription "Praga caput regni"

Wolmut finished the work. On the ground floor were magnificently furnished living quarters, on the first floor, a big dance hall. Today art exhibitions of the National Gallery are held in the Belvedere. The rhythm of the light arcades, the magnificent sculptural decorations and the gracious lines of the roof make the Royal Summer Palace a pearl of Prague architecture.

In front of the summer palace stands an outstanding work in bronze, the Singing Fountain, on which drops falling on the metal produce the illusion of musical sounds. The fountain was designed by the North Italian artist Francesco Terzi and cast by the Prague metal-caster Tomáš Jaroš in 1558—1568.

In the grounds of the Royal Garden we can find to this day the monumental Renaissance building of the Ball-Games Court (Míčovna) built by Bonifaz Wolmut and Ulrico Aostalis in North Italian Palladian style in 1567—1569. And there is the former Lions' Court (Lví dvůr) where wild animals were kept until 1740. The Neo-Classical motifs of the semi-columns and arcades, characteristic of the buildings designed by this architect, were further developed in the 17th century in the Baroque Hradčany palaces.

The Golden Lane at Prague Castle came into existence at the end of the 16th century when the royal sharpshooters began to build their dwellings into the Castle fortifications. The small houses were also the homes of the goldsmiths of Rudolph II, from whom the little lane got its name.

In the Baroque period the Royal Garden was adapted in the French Geometrical Style, but during the Empire period it was changed into an English park, and such it has remained to this day. When the building of the Royal Summer Palace opened the way to the Renaissance at Prague Castle, the Bohemian noblemen began to build one palace after another in its close vicinity. The cause for this was a large fire in 1541, which destroyed large parts of the Castle and the Lesser Town.

At the western edge of the Castle spur Schwarzenberg Palace was built; originally it was known as Lobkowicz Palace and has retained its Renaissance character to this day. At the present time it houses the collections of the Military History Museum. The palace was built by the Italian master Augustin for the Supreme Burgrave of Prague Jan of Lobkowicz in the years 1545—1563. The massive smooth walls, with simple diamond ornament in sgraffito, the receding lunette balustrade of North Italian type, the Renaissance bipartite windows and stressed Renaissance gables leave a mighty and dignified impression and convincingly represent the growing power of the Bohemian aristocracy in the second half of the 16th century.

On the opposite side of Hradčany Square, on the site of today's Archbishop's Palace (Arcibiskupský palác), the Royal Secretary Florián of Gryspek built himself a palace. Opposite St Vitus' Cathedral a vast palace was built for Squire Vilém of Rožmberk by Court builder Ulrico Aostalis. (Later it became the Baroque Institute of Noblewomen.) The onion roofs of its little towers with their curves and horizontals enhance the outline of the Castle, and the palace is a striking counterpoint to the Gothic verticals.

Ferdinand I entrusted his son Ferdinand of Tyrol with the supervision of the royal buildings at Prague Castle and after his experiences with the Bohemian resistance in

Schwarzenberg Palace on Hradčany Square, built by Agustino Vlach in the years 1545—1563. Today the Military History Museum

A Renaissance cassette ceiling in Schwarzenberg Palace, with a painting of the Judgment of Paris, c. 1580

1547, named him viceroy and gave him extensive rights. Prague thus once again became a residential town, though second-rate with a small Archduke's court and few international contacts; but the town gained perspective with the revival of public and social life and more commercial activity.

Ferdinand of Tyrol had plans worked out for a Star Summer Palace (Hvězda) for his wife Filipina Welser, the beautiful daughter of an Augsburg banker, with whom he lived in mésalliance. The palace derived its name from its shape of a six-sided star. This first monumental piece of secular architecture in the environs of Prague was erected close to an old trade route at the western edge of the town by Court builders B. Wolmut and H. Tyrol. Though the interior decorations of finely modelled Italian stucco were not finished everywhere, the Star Summer Palace is an outstanding monument, showing both period individualism, a positive attitude to nature and the variety and inventiveness of Renaissance art. Since 1968 it has become a museum of the writer Alois Jirásek and the painter Mikoláš Aleš.

The Renaissance façade of the Gothic House "At the Minute" on the Old Town Square with sgraffito decorations showing biblical and mythological scenes and allegories of the Virtues

Detail of the Renaissance sgraffito on the façade
of the House "At the Minute"

Rudolphinian Prague

The Renaissance re-building of Prague under Ferdinand I took place after a big fire in the Lesser Town and in Hradčany in 1541. It was the preface to the culminating period during the reign of Rudolph II. The fire broke out in a house called Bastion on the Lesser Town Square (today part of Sternberg Palace on the northern side of the square) and destroyed the larger part of the Lesser Town and to a large extent also Prague Castle. Apart from valuable monuments the fire destroyed the Land Rolls, in which records of the law courts had been inscribed from the 13th century on.

Whole families of Italian builders and stone masons were employed on the re-building of the Lesser Town. Most of them had come from Northern Italy and settled in the Lesser Town in the first half of the 16th century, where they lived in the vicinity of today's Vlašská street. A number of Renaissance houses in this street to this day recall the Italian artists and craftsmen who made Prague their home. One such house belonged to the imperial Court architect Ulrico Aostalis, another was the Italian Hospital — today Casa d'Italia — opposite Lobkowicz Palace.

The Renaissance courtyard of the Old Mayor's House in Na můstku street in the Old Town, originally the seat of the Royal Magistrate in the Gall Town, founded c. 1234 and rebuilt in Renaissance style c. 1588

The arcaded Late Renaissance court of Teufel House in Melantrichova street in the Old Town (No. 463) from the early 17th century

Of these Renaissance houses on the Lesser Town Square there survives, in the corner opposite St Thomas' Church, the representative Renaissance Lesser Town Hall. Otherwise after later reconstruction and adaptations only the House "At the Golden Lion" (U zlatého lva) has retained its original character. Today a snug little wine cellar "At the Patron's" (U mecenáše) survives. Several attractive Renaissance gables can also be found in Mostecká street, including the ostentatious Saxon House (Saský dům) by the Lesser Town Bridge Tower. The façades of the Renaissance houses in Nerudova street are hidden under later Baroque adaptations with stucco decorations.

Ferdinand I's son Maximilian II (1564—1576) did not make Prague his residential town. During his reign building construction continued, under Court architect B. Wolmut,

The Renaissance House "At the Three Ostriches" below the taller Lesser Town Bridge Tower was built in 1597. It derived its name from a former owner, Jan Fux, a merchant dealing in ostrich feathers. In 1714 an Armenian, Deodatus the Damascene, opened the first Prague coffee-house here.

on the Ball-Games Court in the Royal Garden and on the Castle itself (the stables in the second forecourt). But intricate religious relations crystallized in new form after the emergence of Martin Luther in Germany in 1517.

The Bohemian Utraquists first behaved in irresolute manner towards the German Reformation, but in 1524 the Old Prague Utraquists used the religious questions as an excuse for a political rising in the town and the persecution of adherents to the Lutheran faith, the Neo-Utraquists. Even though Ferdinand I later took measures against them, the number of adherents grew until, at a conference in 1575, the Bohemian non-Catholic religious parties — mainly the Lutherans, the Neo-Utraquists and the Czech Brethren — agreed on the Czech Confession, which was to replace the outmoded Basle Compacts. A bronze memorial plaque on the Lesser Town Hall recalls where

Portrait of Emperor Rudolph II, etching by J. Sadeler, 1606

The Renaissance Star Summer Palace was built by Juan Maria Aostalis and Giovanni Luchese in 1555—1556 according to a design by Archduke Ferdinand of the Tyrol in the shape of a six-pointed star. Italian artists worked the fine stucco with subjects of ancient mythology. Today the Alois Jirásek and Mikoláš Aleš Museum

Late Gothic vaults in the Church Na Karlově, the work of the Court architect Bonifaz Wolmut, 1575

the Czech Confession was written — a new confession of faith of the Bohemian Protestants.

But on pressure from the Pope and the Spanish branch Maximilian II refused to confirm this Czech Confession. His son Emperor Rudolph II (1566—1611) resisted for thirty years until the Bohemian Protestant Estates, in a critical political situation, forced him to confirm their religious freedom in a special Letter of Majesty. Rudolph's Letter of Majesty of 1609 basically approved the Czech Confession and gave non-Catholics extensive religious and political rights. This occurred in the last years of the Emperor's reign when enemies in Hungary and among the Austrian Estates, under the leadership of his brother Matthias, faced the ageing and sick monarch. Since only the Czechs could save Rudolph's throne at this perilous moment, the Letter of Majesty was to be their reward. It did not bring them the longed-for peace. On the contrary, its deliberate disregard by the Catholic viceroy led to a second anti-Habsburg rising after Rudolph's death and was the prelude and first act of the Thirty Years' War. This changed conditions in Europe but nowhere as radically as in the Czech Lands.

Previous to this, Bohemia enjoyed a quarter century of economic prosperity, and social, cultural and particularly artistic life flourished greatly. Emperor Rudolph II was the first of the Habsburg monarchs who raised Prague to residential status, and from 1584 until his death he actually lived at Prague Castle. This was the second and last time that the "Head of the Kingdom" — as the gold inscription above the Renaissance window of the Old Town Hall of 1520 proudly proclaims — became the capital city of the Empire and fully availed itself of all the advantages arising from this.

The town filled with foreigners, aristocratic courtiers, noblemen from all parts of Europe, exotic merchants, who brought along expensive and luxury goods for their rich customers. A multitude of people formed the essential following of an imperial Court, including artists, scientists, inventors, craftsmen of all manner of professions and the unavoidable sharlatans and impostors. Rudolph's Prague Court attracted enterprising people from afar; the town grew with the immigrants and became rich with the new social activities, and the inflow of money which the wealthy foreigners brought with them.

More than two centuries after Emperor Charles IV Prague once again lived through

Painted Renaissance ceiling of wood in the Burgrave's House at Prague Castle from the 16th century. Today the House of Czechoslovak Children

a golden era. It was no mere chance that at the Rudolphinian time the epithet "Golden Prague" was used for the first time, as it reflected the glitter and magnificence of the imperial Court in Prague and its magnificent art collections.

For Emperor Rudolph II had similar leanings as Charles IV. Both were passionate collectors of art, but while the great Luxemburg Emperor was still a predominantly mystical soul, a Gothic admirer of holy relics, the pleasure-seeking Renaissance Rudolph II developed his passions to an unheard-of degree at the very end of the Renaissance period. He made Prague Castle one of the greatest museums of world art.

Compared with Charles IV, the founder of the Gothic metropolis, Rudolph concentrated on the Castle, which he furnished with every comfort and enlarged with new halls for his collections. He preferred to live with his Court in the Royal Garden with the Belvedere, the Ball-Games Court, a shooting range, a riding school and the Lions' Court like Italian noblemen, and he divided his time among his delight in works of art, engagement in fashionable sports and talking to scholars, medical men, astronomists, astrologists, or alchemists. Rudolph, unlike Charles IV, lacked the wisdom of a ruler and diplomat. For that reason the end of his political career was tragic-comic.

Renaissance wrought metal grating of 1560 on the fountain on the Little Square, Old Town

Rudolph himself embodied in exemplary manner the period type of a decadent person, who under very favourable conditions of time and location fully and consistenly applied his aesthetic leanings and the cultural ambitions of a refined aristocratic intellectual living at the conclusion of one spiritual and artistic period.

The art of the second half of the 16th century in exaggeratedly polished form, expressiveness, or deformation represented a reaction to the inner crisis of Man, whose reliance on traditional spiritual values had broken down. It is conventionally labelled by the not very suitable term of Mannerism. The most advantageous setting for its development was the Court enclave, since it was here, in a highly sensitive and over-intellectual atmosphere, that the sharpest and most profound spiritual crises occurred. And since Mannerism as one expression of the crisis of feudal society was not basically a spiritual reaction to the Renaissance it found the ground prepared even in the countries to the north of the Alps, where Gothic feeling survived smoothly into the 16th century. Both these prerequisites were ideally merged in Rudolphinian Prague,

The Grand Priory Mill on the Čertovka Stream with a large wooden wheel is the last of the Old Prague mills.

The Late Renaissance Hradčany Town Hall was built by Caspar Oemichen in the years 1601 — 1604. Today it is a private house.

▶
Smiřický Palace on the Lesser Town Square, originally Renaissance from the early 17th century, reconstructed in Late Baroque style by architect Josef Jäger after 1763. Here, in May 1618, the second Prague Defenestration was plotted, which caused the Thirty Years' War to break out.

Martinic Palace on Hradčany Square

which, for that reason, grew into the most important centre of international Mannerism at the beginning of the 17th century.

By contrast to Charles and his grandfather Ferdinand I, who undertook extensive building construction, Rudolph II concentrated on other types of art, painting, sculpture, and arts-and-crafts. In this respect we might compare Rudolph with Wenceslas II, whose Court culture in its over-cultivation with erotic undertones was very close to Rudolphinian Mannerism.

Rudolph had two main halls built at Prague Castle for his immense collections, the Gallery and the Spanish Hall, situated in the northern wing of the present second courtyard. Here he gradually amassed some three thousand pictures by leading world masters, some two and a half thousand sculptures and thousands of various objects of craftsmanship and small sculpture.

The Italian Chapel of Our Lady in the Clementinum in Karlova street in the Old Town by an unknown Roman architect, 1590—1600, the first sign of Roman Baroque in Prague

The portal of the House "At the Two Golden Bears" at the corner of Melantrichova and Kožná streets in the Old Town, end of 16th century, the most beautiful Renaissance house portal in Prague

Rudolph's Gallery contained examples of important works by all great Italian masters, such as Leonardo da Vinci, Michelangelo, Raphael, Giorgione, Titian and Correggio, Dutch art headed by Pieter Bruegel the Elder, German Renaissance masters, particularly Albrecht Dürer, Hans Holbein the Younger and Lucas Cranach. Apart from pictures the Emperor collected statues of Antiquity (he owned the famous Illioneus, now in the Munich Glyptothek) Greek and Roman gems and medals, coins, mosaics, Renaissance engravings, clocks, natural science apparatuses and also — in accordance with the taste of the time — a variety of naturalia and curiosities, among them twenty-one rhinoceros horns. The value of the collections was estimated in 1619 to amount to 17 million Gilders, and it included, in addition, a library, with many illuminated manuscripts and a collection of precious weapons.

[123 Part of Rudolph's collection was actually made by his Court artists who constantly surrounded the Emperor. He summoned them to his Court from the whole of Europe, maintained friendly relations with them and showed them great favours. Artists in whom he was especially interested were raised to the nobility. Some of them were entrusted with the task of business agents in the acquisition of new works for the collections. And when it was at times impossible to acquire a desired original the Court artists made copies for Rudolph.

A leading position among them was held by the Dutch painter Bartholomeus Spranger, who settled in Prague, married and founded a family. He made his home in Nerudova street in the Lesser Town and left his last will and testament in the Czech language.

The Court group of Mannerists included the Dutch painters and graphic artists Roeland Savery, Jan Bruegel, Joris Hoefnagel, Egidius Sadeler and Pieter Stevens, a Swiss painter Josef Heintz, a German Hans von Aachen, and for a short time the famous Italian Mannerist Guiseppe Arcimboldo. Prague did not suit him and with the Emperor's permission Arcimboldo went back to his native Italy, where he received his annual pay as Court painter, a position he retained.

The Royal Tomb in St Vitus' Cathedral, with figures of Ferdinand I, his wife Anne and son Maximilian II on the lids, the work of the Dutch sculptor Alexander Collin, 1564—1589

Late Renaissance tomb of Rabbi Jehuda Löwe (died 1609) on the Old Jewish Cemetery

Late Renaissance tomb of the famous astronomer of Emperor Rudolph II, Tycho de Brahe, in the Church of Our Lady-before-Týn, dated 1601

Apart from painters there were sculptors at Rudolph's Court headed by the outstanding Dutch Mannerist Adriaen de Vries, goldsmiths (Jan Vermeyen), glass-cutters (Karl Lehmann), gem-cutters (M. Kraetsch) and polishers of gemstones (the Miseroni brothers), clock-makers (Jošt Burgi), and makers of scientific instruments (Erasmus Habermehl).

Rudolphinian Prague acquired fame as a centre of scientific studies. At the Prague Court were mysterious figures of alchemists and magicians such as Edgar Kelley of England. Alongside the showy experiments of alchemists and the fantastic ideas of astrologers research was carried out by world famous astronomers, who on recommendation of Tadeus Hájek of Hájek, the head of the imperial alchemists' workshop, were invited by Rudolph to his Court.

Hercules, bronze statue by Adriaen de Vries, c. 1625. National Gallery, Prague

126]

Epitaph of the Prague goldsmith Müller with a picture of the Resurrection by B. Spranger, Court Painter to Rudolph II. The painting dates from 1588. National Gallery, Prague

[127

Vladislav Hall at the Time of Emperor Rudolph II with Sadeler's Booth, detail of an etching by Egidius Sadeler, 1607

The Danish astronomer Tycho de Brahe carried out his last experimental observations in Prague. He published his book here in 1602 and died in the city. A Renaissance tomb in Týn Church to this day recalls the place where the bodily remains of this famous man were laid to rest. Even more important was the visit by Johann Kepler, who in Prague discovered the law of the movement of heavenly bodies, to be named in his honour, which he published in book form here. Even if Kepler, as part of his function, had to work out the Emperor's astrological horoscopes — Rudolph II was very superstitious and in his old age increasingly timid — with his calculations of the movement of heavenly bodies Kepler opened up a new epoch in scientific astronomy.

128]

In Prague in 1600 a surgeon, Dr J. Jesenius, held his first public dissection. He later became Rector of Charles University and was one of those executed on the Old Town Square in 1621.

Music at Rudolph's Court contributed to the remarkable breadth of Prague cultural life. Leading representatives of European music of the time, musicians from the Netherlands, France and Germany, met in Prague and their work, like that in the fine arts, opened the way to the Baroque period.

During the twenty-five years of its existence Rudolphinian Prague came to assume a leading place among European cultural centres. Around 1600 its importance rested in the fact that Rudolph's Court managed to achieve a temporary coexistence of Italian

Glass goblet with engraved ornaments by Caspar Lehmann. Museum of Decorative Arts in Prague

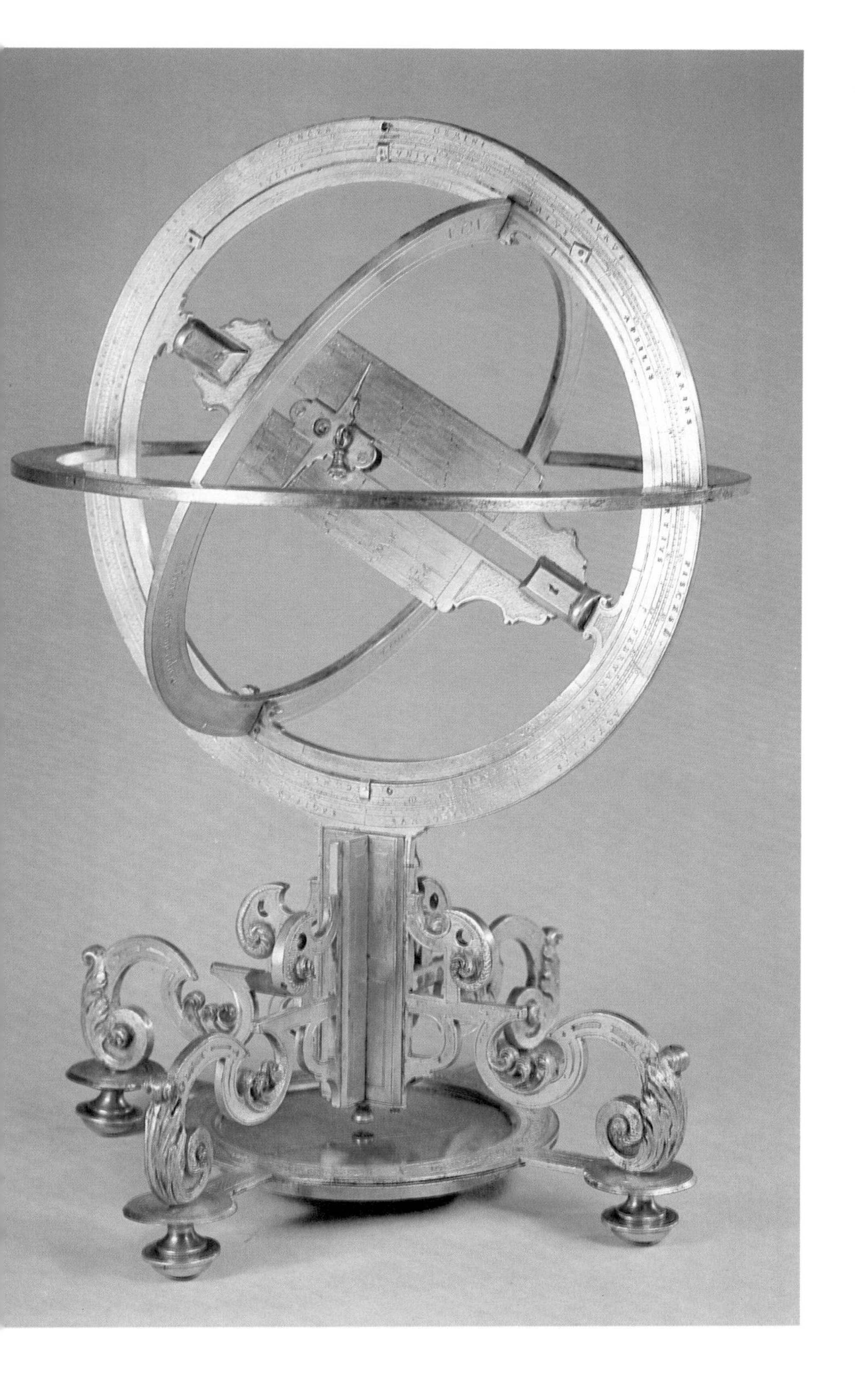

Astrolabe by E. Habermehl. Museum of Decorative Arts in Prague

View of Prague Castle and the Lesser Town at the Renaissance Period, etching by J. Kozel and M. Peterle, 1562

and northern currents of Late Renaissance painting in the framework of pre-Baroque Mannerism, which in many ways determined the original character of Czech Baroque art. The main merit in this must be ascribed to the Emperor himself, the great collector, patron of the arts and supporter of artists.

The strange Rudolph, who never married, loved art and antiquities, had the works of goldsmiths inset with gemstones. He had new Coronation Jewels made, which were even more magnificent than those ordered by Charles IV in the 14th century.

And the town below the Castle gained by the presence of the art-loving Emperor, although relations between the ruler and the town were not as favourable and close as during the reign of Charles IV. The Renaissance façade of the burgher's house "At the Minute" (U minuty) dates from Rudolph's period. It stands adjacent to the Old Town Hall and is decorated with sgraffito on antique, biblical and allegorical themes. At the time one of the most beautiful Renaissance portals in Prague was built on the House "At the Two Golden Bears" (U dvou zlatých medvědů) in Melantrichova street. The memorial plaque on this house recalls that the Roving Reporter Egon Erwin Kisch was born here. Emperor Rudolph II also improved the coat-of-arms of the Prague Guild of Painters with the express addendum that it was not to refer to craftsmen but only to painters.

View of Prague from Petřín Hill, oil on wood by Lucas van Valckenborch, c. 1580. Museum of the City of Prague

View of Vyšehrad and Podskalí in the Renaissance Period, detail from an engraving by J. Wechter after a drawing by Philipp van den Bossche, published by E. Sadeler in 1606

King Frederick of the Palatinate Fleeing from Prague
in 1620 after the Battle of the White Mountain, detail o
a woodcut by K. Bendl of 1630 in the choir gallery
of St Vitus' Cathedral

The high appreciation of works of art, stimulated by the Renaissance cult of the aesthetic, could not remove the remnants of the Middle Ages that continued under the Renaissance façades with their antique sgraffito. These trends showed in the disproportions of the Church of St Roch (sv. Roch), at the corner of Strahov Monastery which Rudolph had built in 1603. A strange shape came into being, on which Gothic again took predominance over the Renaissance style.

The situation in Rudolph's Prague at the turn of the 16th to the 17th century was complicated; great contradictions maintained tension in the basically medieval town, drunk with the luxury of the Imperial Court, and imbued with German Lutheranism and the Spanish spirit of the Jesuits; it was a town in which various European languages were spoken. All this is characterized by one other church structure which was finished in 1600. It is the Italian Chapel (Vlašská kaple) built in Karlova street near the Jesuit Church of St Saviour (sv. Salvátor) by Italian builders and stone masons. Its eliptical ground plan and the Roman character of this small, yet monumentally felt building seems to anticipate the arrival of a new style, during which Prague experienced years of its most profound moral decline and highest artistic development — Baroque.

Baroque Prague

View of the Old Town with Charles Bridge, detail of an etching by Václav Hollar, 1636

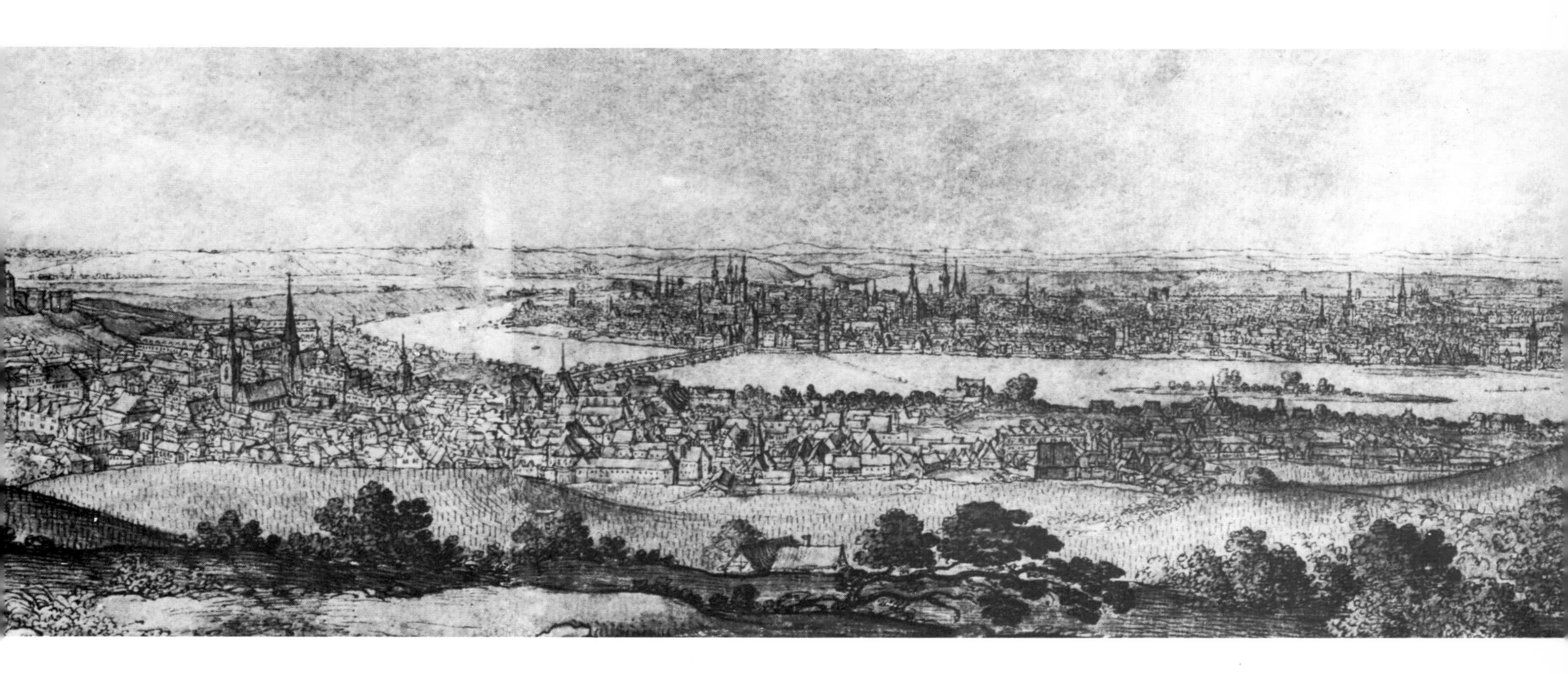

Sala Terrena of the Wallenstein Garden, designed by architect Giovanni Pieroni in 1624—1627

The Victory of the Habsburgs and the Counter-Reformation

Emperor Rudolph II became ever stranger and odd and rancorous in his old age. He would not accept capitulation before his brother Matthias and the Bohemian Estates and tried one final time to change conditions. He summoned the mercenary army of Colonel Ramée from Passau to Bohemia who in 1611 conquered and looted only in the Lesser Town while the Old Town stood firm.

When the Passau men were forced to flee from Prague the Emperor had no choice but to give up the Crown of Bohemia to Matthias. He did not survive this last defeat for long and died at Prague Castle on 20 January 1612 in the midst of his Collections, deserted by all. With him departed a monarch who by making Prague his residental town had contributed to the exceptional prosperity of the town, which, furthermore, thanks to him, became one of the most magnificent centres of education and art in Europe.

In the first years Emperor Matthias seemed to want to continue the cultural endeavours of his brother, even though on a more limited scale, but the growing opposition of the Bohemian Protestant Estates to his pro-Catholic policy forced him to move to Vienna with his whole Court in the autumn of 1617. With it the imperial offices, the Court nobility and ambassadors left Prague as well as bankers and merchants who were dependent on the royal Court, and Prague Castle ceased to be the permanent residence of the Habsburgs for 300 years until the end of their monarchy in 1918.

The disputes between the Catholics and non-Catholics in Bohemia, which were a reflection of the profound contradictions of feudal society, sharpened in 1618. When the Catholic officials appointed by the Emperor deliberately violated Rudolph's Letter of Majesty, which granted religious freedom to Protestants, and all protests remained vain, the Protestant Estates — in the first place, the nobility — decided to resort to action. On 23 May 1618 they set off to the Castle and threw the two most fanatical Catholic governors out of the windows of the Renaissance palace — the Louis Wing — and this inaugurated the second anti-Habsburg rising. The two governors and their

Albrecht of Wallenstein as Mars, mural painting by Baccio di Bianco c. 1630 in the Great Hall of Wallenstein Palace

scribes, who were by accident thrown out with them, did not suffer great injury, but the enmity between the Bohemian Estates and Emperor Matthias was publically declared.

The Bohemian War lasted two years and was the first phase of the Thirty Years' War; after the German states it, by stages, involved Denmark, Sweden, and France, and later affected the whole of Europe from the south to the Baltic Sea and from the Rhineland to Poland. The struggle of the Bohemian Protestant Estates became part of a much broader and extensive struggle between the Protestant League and the Catholic Union in Germany, between the non-Catholic and the Catholic countries in Europe and, in the end, a dispute on political hegemony among the Great European Powers.

Emperor Matthias died in the spring of 1619, and his nephew Ferdinand became his successor. He won the Imperial Crown fairly easily but had to fight for the throne of Bohemia. The Bohemian Protestant Estates rejected him as King and in his place chose Frederick, the Elector of the Palatinate. They assumed that his royal election would ensure them aid from the German Protestants, whose Union was headed by

The Santa Casa in the Loretto, the work of Giovani Orsi and Andrea Alli, 1626—1631, a copy of the alleged house of the Virgin which the angels are said to have moved from Nazareth to the Loretto

Diamond monstrance (with 6,200 diamonds), the most valuable work in the Loretto Treasure, made by Viennese goldsmiths in 1698 to a design by the architect Johann Bernhard Fischer of Erlach

Frederick. And they expected a good deal from Frederick's wife since Queen Elizabeth was the daughter of King James I of England, who as a Stuart belonged to the anti-Catholic camp. Unfortunately none of these expectations — and many others — turned out correct. And when Emperor Ferdinand won over to his side the Electors of Bavaria and Saxony and their joint army defeated the soldiers of the Bohemian Estates in a brief battle at the White Mountain outside Prague on 8 November 1620, the Bohemian War ended in the triumph of the Habsburgs.

We can find few examples in history when one unfortunate battle decided the fate of a nation for three hundred years. When the Bohemian Protestant Estates surrendered voluntarily to the Emperor after the Battle of the White Mountain and asked for mercy, they had no idea what was in store for them and with them the whole Czech nation. The Jesuits had roused anti-Reformation fanaticism in Emperor Ferdinand II which linked up with the inborn Habsburg imperialism and longing for absolute power. He decided that the resisting heretics among the Czechs should be turned into humble and obedient Catholics. And in the first place he determined he would definitively break the economic might of the Bohemian towns and suppress the political freedom of the Estates.

The execution of the twenty-seven leaders of the anti-Habsburg rising took place on the Old Town Square on 21 June 1621. There were seventeen burghers and of these fifteen men of Prague. This was to frighten the Czech nation; fines and confiscations were to reduce the country to beggars financially. Those who refused to adopt the Catholic faith were forced to emigrate and leave all property behind. Thus Bohemia lost one quarter of its population, apart from the nobility the richest and best educated strata of burghers, who preferred the uncertain fate of exile to giving up the faith of their ancestors.

In 1627 Ferdinand II proclaimed a new Constitution of the Kingdom of Bohemia, which legalized the victory of the Habsburgs and ensured their hegemony in the Bohemian state for the future. Catholicism became the only official religion permitted, and the ecclesiastics were awarded the leading place, ahead of the nobility. The Habsburgs became hereditary Kings of Bohemia on the male and female side, all legislature was directly in the hands of the monarch, while the Diet was allowed to discuss only proposals by the King. The King claimed the right to convey laws to the population, acknowledged German alongside Czech as official language and abolished the political power of the towns, which altogether were given one vote in the Diet. So it can be said that Ferdinand II managed to re-implement fully the old Habsburg political credo: to enforce the monarch's absolutism, strengthen the Catholic Church and weaken the towns.

Religious freedom and tolerance, for which the Czech had, without success, striven since the 15th century, was replaced by the radical Counter-Reformation, which began with such brutal persecution of the non-Catholics that we can find no comparison

The interior of the Jesuit Church of St Ignatius on Charles Square, built to a project by the architect Carlo Lurago in 1665—1670

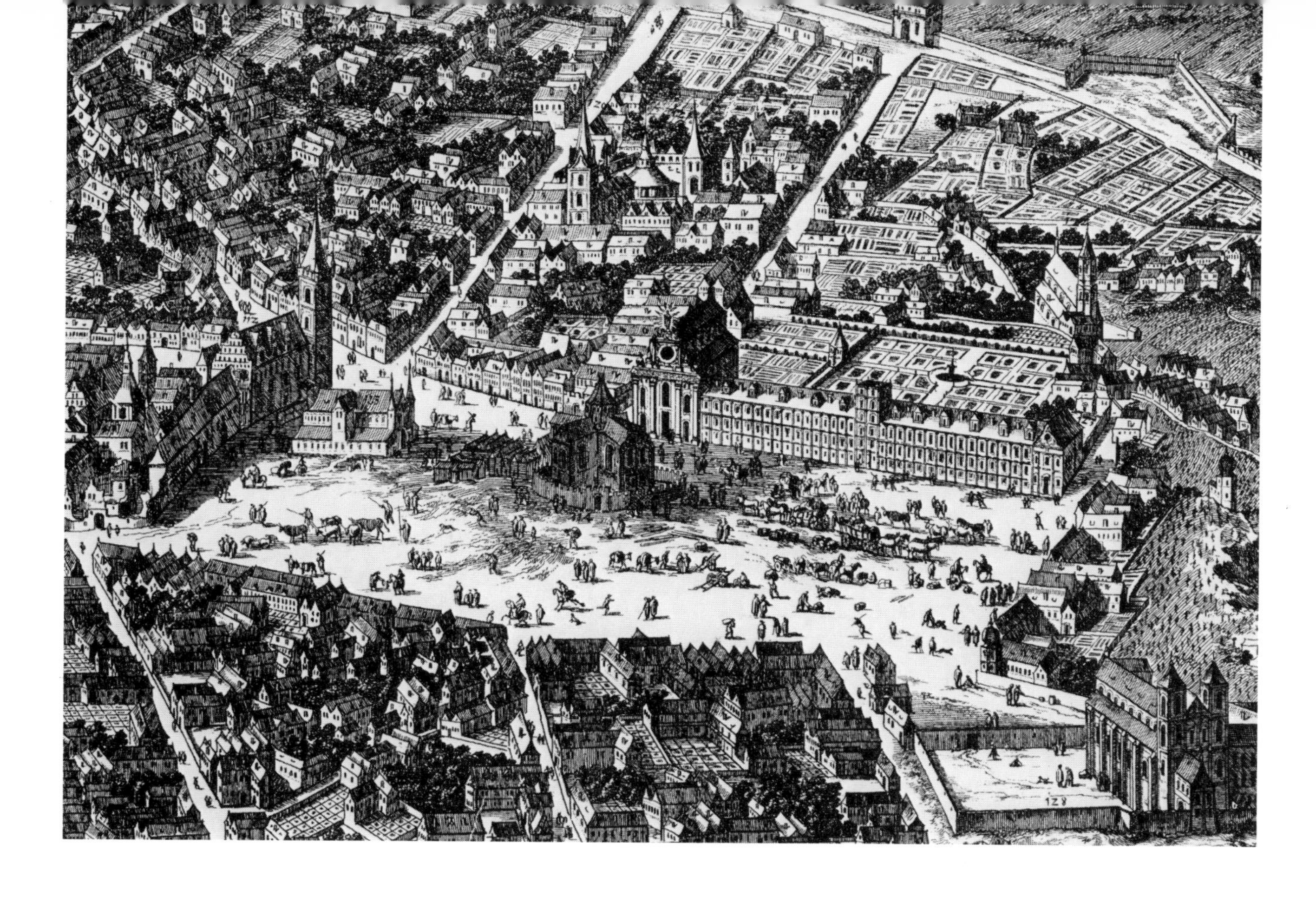

View of Charles Square, detail of the Prospect of Prague which Coenraet Decker engraved after a drawing by Forpert van Ouden and Jan van Ghellen, printed in Vienna in 1685

in Europe for centuries. The Jesuits proclaimed religious tolerance as the source of all sins and compromise in faith the greatest of crimes. In the Counter-Reformation persecution fell heaviest on the serfs, who were not permitted to move away but were ordered by brute force to adopt the Catholic faith.

The decline of the Czech Lands was hastened by the Thirty Years' War with accompanying features such as dues for keeping the armies, robbery, looting, burning down of towns and villages. No wonder that at the end of the Thirty Years' War there were a mere million inhabitants in Bohemia out of the original population of two to three million and that Prague was a half deserted town with thousands of looted homes.

Early Baroque Architecture and Aristocratic Palaces

Emigration and widespread confiscation of the property of Prague burghers and their general impoverishment formed, on the other hand, ideal prerequisites for the successful onset of Baroque architecture. They provided sufficient space for projects of vast palaces as favoured by the new Bohemian nobility and for monumental Jesuit colleges and monastery buildings of the new religious Orders, who found advantageous conditions for their existence in Prague after 1620.

[139

After the defeat of the Rising of the Czech Bohemian Estates the Baroque style thus became the victorious art form of the Habsburgs, the Counter-Reformation and Catholic nobility, in the first place, and the imperial generals who subdued Prague and Bohemia. The new style was to emphasize for all to see that conditions had radically changed and that there was no choice but to adapt or at least become accustomed to the way of life of the southern Catholics.

The first buildings had gone up in the new style even before the anti-Habsburg rising. Emperor Matthias built the Matthias Gate as the main entrance to the Castle according to plans by his Court architect Giovanni M. Fillipi in 1614. To this day it leads from the first courtyard into the next one. It is a paradox that apart from this gate the first Prague Baroque church was a church of the German Lutherans, who built it in the Lesser Town in 1611—1613 and consecrated it to the Holy Trinity. When conditions changed the Emperor personally decided it was to be given to the Spanish Order of the Bare-Footed Carmelites — whose name is borne by the adjacent Karmelitská street — who consecrated it to Our Lady-Victorious (Panny Marie Vítězné). In 1636—1644 a new entrance façade was financed by the Spanish General of the Imperial Army at the White Mountain, Don Baltazar de Marradas. The entrance to the church had first been from the west, as was the tradition, and its remains are the portal that today forms the gateway to the right of the present-day façade.

The originally Lutheran church became an important Lesser Town centre of the Catholic Counter-Reformation and received particular support from the immigrant foreign nobility. The wax figurine of the Prague Child Jesus is to this day kept in its interior.

Michna Palace in the Lesser Town, built probably after a plan by Francesco Caratti in 1640—1650

Černín Palace at Hradčany, built to a design by the architect Francesco Caratti in 1669—1697, portico and balconies added by the architect Anselmo Lurago in 1747. The most monumental palace in Prague is now the Ministry of Foreign Affairs of the Czechoslovak Socialist Republic.

It is a little work of the Spanish Renaissance, which Polyxena of Lobkowicz gave to the Carmelites in 1628. She was a leading representative of the local Catholic nobility, and had become famous by saving the defenestrated governors in 1618. The little statue, one of the most remarkable curiosity of Prague, is worshipped in particular in Latin America. It is deposited in a silver case, made by the Lesser Town goldsmith Jan Pakeni in 1741 and stands on a marble side altar made by franz Martin Lauermann in 1776 and adorned with statues by Peter Prachner.

Above the three Early Baroque altars with their solemn contrast of black and gold we can find outstanding pictures by the leading painter of Prague Baroque Petr Brandl. In the large crypts below the church many secular supporters of the Order (besides the Carmelites) are buried in open coffins, and the dry air has preserved their bodies in remarkable manner.

Characteristic of the first period of Prague Baroque after 1620 are palaces of two noble Catholic nouveau-richs, who built them during the Thirty Years' War, Albrecht of Wallenstein, and his companion in the royal finance commission, Pavel Michna of Vacínov.

Albrecht of Wallenstein was Imperial General, and he acquired an immense fortune by financial transactions with the confiscated estates of the non-Catholic nobility, a suitable marriage and as remuneration for his military services during the Thirty Years' War. Emperor Ferdinand II first showed Wallenstein great favour, made him Generallissimo, Count of Frýdlant and Mecklenburg with the title of Admiral, but when

The interior of the Gothic Church of St James in the Old Town, later adapted in Baroque style by J. Š. Pánek, 1689—1702. After St. Vitus' Cathedral the second longest church in Prague

Wallenstein — by nature a calculating adventurer without principles — began to execute a policy of his own and came to terms even with the enemy, the Emperor had him assassinated at Cheb on 2 February 1634.

But before that Albrecht of Wallenstein had had time to build the extensive complex of his palace (Valdštejnský palác) in the Lesser Town, which in size and monumentality could favourably compete with Prague Castle itself. Without regard to existing communications, town fortifications and walls, the owners of twenty-three houses, three gardens and one brickworks, the Count of Frýdlant built himself an estate in the midst of the town, in a densely inhabited district.

The palace was separated by a new square and a garden wall from the town settlement, and formed an enclosed domain, out of bounds to the surrounding world. The main interest centred on the inner parts, the garden sala terrena and the luxurious furnishings of the interior. The vast piece of architecture, basically a Late Renaissance palace with Baroque details, came into being in the years 1623—1630 according to a design by the Italian builders Andrea Spezzi and Nicola Sebregondi under the supervision of the Count's building specialist Giovanni Pieroni.

Even if basically an Italian palace, certain motifs — portals and niches in particular — do not deny their northern origin. The main wing comprises the Great Hall, which takes up two storeys and is adorned with stucco vaulting and a ceiling picture of Albrecht of Wallenstein as the god of war Mars on a triumphal chariot. It is the work of the Italian painter Baccio di Bianco (c. 1630). There is a chapel consecrated to St Wenceslas decorated with stucco and mural paintings by the same artist.

The most beautiful Baroque tomb in Prague is that of the High Chancellor Jan Václav Vratislav of Mitrovice in the Church of St James in the Old Town. It was designed by the Viennese architect Johann Bernhard Fischer of Erlach and built by the Prague sculptor Ferdinand Maximilan Brokoff in 1714—1716

The monumental sala terrena in the garden was built by Giovanni Pieroni in the Mannerist style following the pattern of the portico which his namesake designed for the church in Italian Livorno. The ceiling stucco and pictures of the War of Troy were made by Baccio di Bianco. Outside the palace lies the garden with a grotto, fountain, aviary and little fishpond adorned with casts of bronze statues by Adriaen de Vries, the originals of which, culminating Mannerist sculpture, are to this day to be found in the garden of the Swedish castle of Drottningholm near Stockholm, where they were taken as loot by the Swedish General Königsmark in 1648. The grounds of Wallenstein Palace are enclosed at Klárov by the building of a Riding School (Jízdárna), which since 1955 has housed exhibitions of the National Gallery.

In front is the Malostranská Metro station, which sensitively fits into the Baroque setting and is one of the artistically most impressive designs of the Prague underground railway.

Wallenstein personally participated in the building of his palace and himself ordained subjects for the painted decorations. He equipped his palace with its truly royal furnishings — precious Brussels and Oriental tapestries, Italian furniture, leather upholstery, velvet and silk hangings, pictures and precious works of craftsmanship, but he was able to enjoy all this for a mere four years. It may have been that foreboding of the approaching end made him spare no effort to complete the construction work.

Wallenstein Palace is today the seat of the Ministry of Culture of the Czech Socialist Republic. It did not have any exceptional architectural design or artistic value but greatly affected the plan of the Lesser Town and was a harbinger of social changes in that district. Instead of the Gothic and Renaissance dwellings of small craftsmen and traders, there arose a town of great aristocratic palaces and Baroque gardens, which took

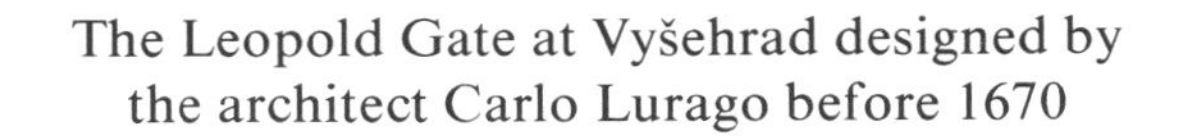

The Leopold Gate at Vyšehrad designed by the architect Carlo Lurago before 1670

The Troja Summer Palace built to a design by J. B. Mathey in 1679—1685, the most beautiful suburban villa of Prague Baroque

the place of the vineyards below the Castle and also covered the slopes below Strahov.

Particularly the immediate vicinity of Wallenstein Palace became an enclave of the aristocracy, who built their palaces here until the late 18th century. Wallenstein Palace set the pattern for a new type of aristocratic town residence in Prague, raised above the surrounding town houses, and their great arrogant challenge embodied the power of victorious feudalism and Catholicism.

The second Early Baroque palace was that of Michna of Vacínov. It took up a relatively large building lot stretching from Karmelitská street to the Čertovka (the Devil's Stream) on Kampa Island. It is not as large but has a more interesting building history and is of a more remarkable architectonic level.

Pavel Michna of Vacínov was a typical Baroque speculator, who, after the victory of the Habsburgs, used financial machinations and war supplies to acquire great property. In 1623 he first bought himself a suburban Renaissance villa, which at the end of 1580 had been built for Count Kinský by the imperial builder Ulrico Aostalis.

Pavel Michna was naturally not satisfied with this Renaissance summmer palace and immediately proceeded to build a new more ostentatious palace, of which, by his death, he had only realized the part with the portal, the riding school and store of army supplies. His son Wenceslas added an eastern garden wing to the Renaissance building in 1640—1650 and made the whole into a palace.

Michna invested in many other building projects, and lack of funds did not permit him to carry out the grandiose structure on the original plans proposed by the gifted Italian architect Francesco Caratti. The northern projections with the rich stucco decorations by Domenico Galli and part of the central section show the precise architectonic layout and the exact graded articulation of the whole façade, the high artistic value of the work, which in style was based on North Italian Mannerism enriched with intense

[145

Roman decorations. As in the case of Wallenstein Palace, here, too, the main artistic interest centred on the garden which was closed to the general public.

Michna Palace became an armoury in 1767, and after the proclamation of the Czechoslovak Republic it became the headquarters of the patriotic physical training organization Sokol and was called Tyrš House (Tyršův dům). Today it serves as Museum of Physical Education and Sport.

Wallenstein and Michna Palaces began a building boom, which, in the second half of the 17th century, after the Thirty Years' War, gave the Lesser Town and Hradčany the character of an aristocratic district.

During the war still Count Rudolph Colloredo, the military Commander of Prague in 1648, began to build a mighty palace at Market Place (Tržiště) on the site of five

The statue of St John of Nepomuk on Charles Bridge, cast in bronze by the Nuremberg metal-caster W. J. Herold in 1683 after a sketch by the Viennese sculptor M. Rauchmüller and a model by Johann Brokoff. The oldest sculpture on the bridge, it served as model for numerous statues of the Saint all over Europe.

houses and vineyards. It had a terraced Baroque garden and an arcaded garden house designed to be seen through the vestibule of the main wing. The terse Early Baroque appearance of the palace, which corresponded to the military character of its builder, was later changed by a more plastic layout of the upper floors, with gables above the windows and niches, for which plans were worked out by the leading Baroque architect Giovanni Alliprandi after 1515. The Italian type garden was admired already in the 17th century and was then a great sight in Prague. Today the palace is called Schönborn and houses the Embassy of the United States of America.

Between Michna Palace and the Monastery of the Knights of Malta in its Baroque adaptation Jan Hertvik Count Nostitz had an imposing palace built in 1658—1660 according to a design by architect Francesco Caratti. It filled the area of two houses and one garden. Its immense block of four wings with an inner courtyard served representative purposes of the High Chamberlain and housed the rich family art collections and the library. The Rococo portal and balconies at the windows of the second floor were added in the second half of the 18th century while the statues of the emperors on

Square of the Knights of the Cross in the Old Town lined by the façade of the Church of the Knights of the Cross (architect J. B. Mathey, 1680—1689) and the front of the Church of St Saviour (1601) with a portico (architect Francesco Caratti, 1651—1653)

Tuscany Palace on Hradčany Square built to a project by J. B. Mathey in 1689—1691

the attic are copies of original works of Michal Josef Brokoff. Only twelve parallel pilasters indicate the original appearance of the palace, in which this Palladian motif appeared for the first time in Prague. The famous Nostitz art gallery is today incorporated in the National Gallery in Prague.

The palace today is used by the Dutch Embassy and the Ministry of Culture of the Czech Socialist Republic. All that remains is the Nostitz Library with many valuable volumes, including illuminated Gothic manuscripts. At the end of the 18th century Josef Dobrovský, the founder of Slavonic and Bohemian studies, was librarian here, and he lived in a garden house in Nostitz Garden on Kampa Island. A statue by Seidan of 1891 pays tribute to this great man of Enlightenment. Until his death in 1980 the house was used by the actor Jan Werich.

The architect Francesco Caratti worked for Michna and Nostitz, and he also designed the largest palace in Prague, Černín Palace. It was begun at Hradčany in 1669 by one of the wealthiest aristocrats of the time, the Imperial Ambassador Humprecht Černín of Chudenice (1628—1682) after his return from Ambassadorship in Venice. The palace grew to such size and had such costly decorations that it almost ruined the Count financially.

Černín first tried out plans by the most famous of Italian Baroque architects Lorenzo Bernini, but without success. He did not come to an agreement with the leading Prague architect Carlo Lurago either. The palace was finally completed by his heirs and was not furnished comfortably until 1718—1720 when French and Dutch tapestries, Chinese upholstery, French furniture, Meissen and Chinese porcelain was imported and leading Prague artists carried out magnificent decorations: architect František Maxmilián Kaňka, sculptor Matthias Bernard Braun (the statues have not survived) and painter Václav Vavřinec Reiner (the fresco above the stairway). The damage the palace suffered during the French occupation of Prague and Prussian bombardment was repaired by Dientzenhofer's son-in-law architect Anselmo Lurago, who, in 1747, added the portals and the portico of the main entrance with a balcony.

The palace could not be kept up financially by the family, and in 1851 it was bought up by the government and turned into barracks. In 1928—1932 it was renovated by architect Pavel Janák to become the Ministry of Foreign Affairs, which it remains to this day.

The exaggerated scale of the building makes Černín Palace the most monumental work of architecture in Prague. Its façade is 150 m long, there are mighty diamond rustics of the ground floor, and the thirty mighty Palladian semi-pillars add great plasticity. They run across two floors to the main cornice, making Černín Palace a dignified counterpart to the Castle. Here Prague Neo-Classical palace architecture derived from the North Italian Renaissance reached its climax. The northern garden façade with two loggias reveals Caratti's Palladian inspiration in his work as architect.

Garden front of Lobkowicz Palace in the Lesser Town built in the years 1703—1707 after a design by the architect Giovanni Alliprandi. Today the Embassy of the Federal Republic of Germany

The Expansion of the Jesuits

In the second half of the 17th century the Church Orders, primarily the Jesuits, undertook feverish building construction after having acquired immense property following the victory of the Counter-Reformation. The oldest seat of the Prague Jesuits, whom Ferdinand I had summoned to the town in 1556, was the Old Town bank of the River Vltava near Charles Bridge in the former Dominican monastery. The Dominicans, at that time, were given the deserted convent of the Poor Clares at Na Františku by way of restitution.

For such an expanding Order as the Jesuits the medieval monastery and Gothic Church of St Clement was insufficient. Already during the reign of Rudolph II they began to build a new Church of St Saviour, which, during the Thirty Years' War, was given a tribune above the side aisles and stucco decorations, and immediately after the war a cupola was added and an ostentatious portico with the motif of a triumphal arch, richly adorned with stucco (by Domenico Galli) and stone statues (by Johann Georg Bendl).

The last two works — the dome and the portico — were probably designed once again by architect Francesco Caratti, the well-known designer of Early Baroque palaces of

Sternberg Palace on Hradčany Square. Works of modern French sculpture in the Collections of the National Gallery in the garden of Sternberg Palace

the aristocracy. According to his plans the Jesuits began building an immense college in 1653, the biggest building complex in Prague after Prague Castle — built on the site of the old Dominican monastery, three churches, two gardens and thirty-two burghers' houses.

The Clementinum, called after the original Monastery Church of St Clement, a system of buildings, two churches, three chapels around four courtyards, was still under construction in the first third and its interior was furnished after the middle of the 18th century. Its oldest part is the three-storey Early Baroque wing facing Křižovnická street articulated with mighty embossed pillaster orders and decorated with stucco capitals of the emperors, the work of Giovanni Battista Cometa.

The Clementinum became the main operational seat of the Jesuit Counter-Reformationary expansion eastwards. It became an important centre of Baroque culture, particularly when Charles University was merged with the Jesuit University, which took over its property, under the new name of University of Charles-Ferdinand. And it is a certain paradox that it was in Clementinum College, which was involved in the Counter-Reformation aimed against the majority of the Czech nation, that the first predecessor of the Czech National Revivalists grew up: Bohuslav Balbín.

Although he was a Jesuit, he had not lost his awareness of nationality, and as the first true patriot spoke out in defence of his mother tongue and against Germanization. He was praised for this by the spiritual leader of the Czech in exile, who most perfectly represented Czech culture in 17th century Europe, the last Bishop of the Unity of Brethren, Jan Ámos Komenský (Comenius). Balbín seemed to want to show that ardent love for the nation overcomes differences in religious creed, and he educated his pupils in burning patriotism through the work *On the Bohemian State* (O českém státě) by another exile, Pavel Stránský.

The Clementinum, a complex of Early and High Baroque architecture, sculpture and craftsmanship, was adapted for the University (now State) Library of the Czech Socialist Republic in 1928—1930. The Church of St Clement had sculptural decorations from the workshop of M. Braun (1715—1721). In the Early Baroque summer refectory decorated with original stucco there is today a public study; in the Hall of Mirrors, a former chapel built by F. M. Kaňka in 1727, exhibitions and concerts are held, while the Hall of the Jesuit Library (F. M. Kaňka) with ceiling allegories and illusive painting by J. Hiebl (1727) and a number of old globes has retained the remarkable effect of a High Baroque interior.

Under the dome of the Astronomical Tower of 1721—1723 (F. M. Kaňka), adapted in 1748 (by A. Lurago), with a leaden statue of Atlas holding an armillary sphere at the top, a remarkable exhibition is held of astronomical and mathematical instruments, which once belonged to the famous astronomer of Emperor Rudolph II, Tycho de Brahe.

In the Mathematical Hall with Rococo stucco and painted decorations magnificent examples of clocks from the first half of the 18th century are to be found.

In the second half of the 17th century colossal buildings of Jesuit Colleges grew up in the Lesser and the New Town. The foundation stone for the first of these, the New Town College, was laid only five years after the Clementinum (1658—1704) in the place of twenty-three houses and thirteen gardens, and it took up one whole half of the eastern side of Charles Square.

At the northern end the Jesuit Church of St Ignatius (sv. Ignác) was attached, built by Carlo Lurago in 1665—1670. Its layout is that of a typical Jesuit hall with side chapels and tribunes — derived from the Roman church Il Gesu. Its interior is richly adorned with plastically applied stucco and the church rises high above the surrounding houses with its gabled façade and the golden rays of the statue of St Ignatius shining from the top. The tower and portico in front of the façade were added after Lurago's death by Paul Ignaz Bayer (1686—1699). After the dissolution of the Jesuit Order in

1774 the college served as military hospital, and today it is part of the Faculty Hospital of Charles University.

After 1673 a third Prague college was built by the Jesuits in the middle of the Lesser Town Square which was thus divided into two parts. It covered the area of thirteen houses, a school and a Romanesque church. The mighty block of the college, rising high above the houses and palaces around the square, with its terse articulation seems to form an effective contrast to the adjacent façade of the Jesuit Church of St Nicholas, in which for the first time the dynamic forces of High Baroque were fully developed and imprinted upon Prague its characteristic Baroque face.

The Basic Elements of Prague Baroque

Before this could happen Prague underwent a transitional period, in which buildings of excessive size and mass suppressed all around it and replaced the architecture, which had fitted much better into the organism of the Prague Towns in view of its greater sensitivity and artistic taste. But first Prague acquired a new external appearance with the character of a Baroque fortress.

The terraces of Vrtba Garden in the Lesser Town built according to a project by the architect F. M. Kaňka c. 1725. The statues of ancient gods and decorative vases were made in the workshop of Matthias Bernard Braun.

The Church of St Margaret at Břevnov, 1708—1714, built to a project by Christoph Dientzenhofer; after the front of the Church of St Nicholas in the Lesser Town the second building of the illusionistic trend of High Baroque in Prague

The conquest of the New Town by the Swedes at the end of the Thirty Years' War in 1648 showed the weaknesses of the existing defence system of the town so that the Viennese government of Emperor Ferdinand III decided to build modern fortifications in Prague. The old Gothic walls with picturesque towers were pulled down, and in their place there grew up, in the third quarter of the 17th century, new massive brick fortifications with thirty-nine star-shaped bastions.

This transformation affected Vyšehrad most, which lost its medieval character and took on the form of a far too solid and barely attractive citadel, serving entirely military purposes. The civil population had to leave Vyšehrad.

Until the third quarter of the 17th century Baroque architecture in Prague formed a largely uneven set of mutually differing and isolated works. The town was badly affected by the victory of the Habsburgs and the onset of the Counter-Reformation and seemed to oppose a style which was forced upon it by the Catholic aristocracy and the Jesuits. Not until the last quarter of that century did there appear groups of buildings in the unified style of Roman Classicism, which evened out the differences in approach and raised the artistic level of Prague architecture. The artist who introduced this style was Jean Baptiste Mathey, a Burgundy painter, trained as architect in Rome in the circle of the leading representative of French Neo-Classicism, Nicolas Poussin,

[153

where he acquired a sense for the tectonics of a building, the precision of architectural detail, harmony of proportions and the rhythm of the structure.

He was able to apply these qualities to his main work, the Church of St Francis (sv. František) designed for the Order of the Knights of the Cross with a Red Star in the Old Town near Charles Bridge and built in 1680—1689 according to his design by Carlo Lurago. Its noble shape, clear articulation, proportionate size and geometrical cubes with cut away corners enriched the outline of the City of a Hundred Spires with the flowing curve of a cupola, the restrained Old Town counterpart to Dientzenhofer's mighty dome in the Lesser Town. It ideally fills up the small Square of the Knights of the Cross (Křižovnické náměstí), whose intimate space and grandiose Gothic Bridge Tower with a monumental view of the Hradčany panorama and the Lesser Town became enclosed in the Baroque period. Therefore it is one of the most beautiful squares in Prague.

In the perfectly balanced interior of the Church of the Knights of the Cross (Křižovnický kostel), divided by pillasters of dark red Slivenec marble, ten white figures of men and women saints stand in the niches, who in style indicate the transition from Neo-Classicism to radical Baroque. They are the work of the brothers Jeremias and Conrad Süssner of Dresden (before 1690) while Matthias Wenzel Jäckel made the altar and mural paintings in 1705. The presbytery was made by J. K. Liška, the main altar with the picture of the Stigmatization of St Francis, frescoes of angels and allegoric figures date from 1700—1707. The side altar was painted by his step-father, the Silesian painter Michal Willmann (1702) while the large painting of the Last Judgement, a composition of pathetic dynamism in the dome, was made by the leading master of Prague Baroque frescoes, Václav Vavřinec Reiner, in the years 1722 to 1723. This was his second work after the decorations of the stairway in Černín Palace.

The southern side of the Old Town Square with Baroque fronts of originally Gothic houses

The Renaissance House "At the Golden Well" in Karlova street in the Old Town with Baroque stucco reliefs of the Patron Saints that give protection from the pest, made by J. O. Mayer in 1701

Together with the Church of the Knights of the Cross Jean Baptiste Mathey designed the first suburban villa in Prague, the Troja Summer Palace, for Count Václav Vojtěch of Sternberg and his wife Clara of Malzan; it was built in the years 1679—1685. This château was a type of Renaissance Roman villa in monumental Baroque form and in the 18th century its name applied to a whole district on the left bank of the Vltava, where in 1931 the Prague Zoological Garden was laid out.

The architecture of the château, perfectly located in the Vltava valley, displays a Neo-Classical balance and dignified order of pillasters, and has a rich sculptured garden stairways depicting the struggle of gods and Titans, made by the Dresden sculptors Johann Georg and Paul Hermann (1685—1703). The Great Hall has magnificent ceiling and mural paintings, e.g. *In Glorification of the House of Habsburg* by the Antwerp painter Abraham Godyn (1690—1697). The garden surrounding the Summer Palace, which is now being renovated for official purposes of the City of Prague, was the first example of a French Baroque garden in Bohemia.

The third monumental kind of building, an aristocratic palace, was designed by Jean Baptiste Mathey for Count Michal Osvald Thun-Hohenstein in a specially notable place on Hradčany Square facing the entrance to the Castle at the far end. It was built in 1689—1691 by Mare Antonio Canevale as a mighty building with a broad façade divided by two portals with towers on the roof in the manner of the Italian villas. The palace, called Tuscany (Toskánský) after its new owners from 1718 on, enclosed the western side of the square and with its dignified appearance formed a worthy counterpart to the Castle.

Architect Mathey had already contributed to the appearance of Hradčany Square when in 1669—1677 he re-built today's Archbishop's Palace in Baroque style on its eastern side. This early Baroque building period is recalled in the Rococo adaptations on the façade (architect Jan Josef Wirch, 1765) while its central part with the marble portal dates from 1676. The interior furnishings include eight magnificent French tapestries with exotic subjects from the Indies.

At the northern end of the Castle, by the Dusty Bridge (Prašný most) the same architect built the former Royal Summer Riding School around 1694, basically a building of everyday use, which with its vast proportions, double compound pillasters and reliefs on the cornice was upgraded to architecture of artistic merit and today is used for exhibition purposes.

The architectonic creations of J. B. Mathey at the end of the 17th century represent a pre-stage to the origin of a school of art with original features and local characteristics, which we call "Prague Baroque". From the beginning to the middle of the 18th century Prague became a leading centre of Baroque culture and a pleiad of outstanding local and foreign artists, mainly Germans and Italians, were at work here. Most of them soon became naturalized, adapted to the local setting and contributed to the uniqueness and high artistic quality of their collective work — and as such Prague Baroque art leaves its impact upon the spectator to this day.

It took a whole century before Baroque became accepted in Prague. Several generations of artists were needed before the new Italian style, propagated in Bohemia by the Habsburgs and the Counter-Reformatory Church, adapted itself to Prague or — vice versa — before Prague accepted the new style as its own, mastered it and reshaped it to fit into its character.

The Church, and in particular the Jesuits, did a great deal to encourage its spread. They used the sensual and emotional aspects of the new art and heightened the optical and accoustic effect on the believers who were won over by the colourful Catholic liturgy, picturesque processions and Church festivals, whose attractiveness was intensified by melodic folk singing.

In the sphere of publishing, the Jesuits aimed primarily at the imagination and emotional part of the popular soul, when they published religious books in the Czech language for the rural people of Bohemia, who, from the Hussite period on, were interested in reading. By reviving the cult of the old saints of the country, SS Wenceslas, Adalbert and Ludmila, they indirectly supported national consciousness and patriotism, which in substance, however, did not go beyond the limits of feudal local patriotism. Even the new Bohemian nobility could accept this, whose "Bohemianism" did not rest, in many cases, on anything other than the fact that their estates lay in Bohemia.

This Catholic nobility had, in the meantime, acquired a closer relationship to the capital of the Kingdom of Bohemia, which Prague remained even though the King did not reside here, and they were responsible for the unheard-of artistic growth of the town. The ambitions of the nobility and their status made them build ostentatious palaces and attend to their luxurious furnishing even though most of them did not live here for large parts of the year. The high costs of building construction and maintenance of the Prague palaces was well within their means since they had grown rich by confisca-

The Third Courtyard of Prague Castle, etching
by B. B. Werner, 1740

tions and increased their income by exploiting their serfs. And since they were not received at the Court of Vienna with such attention and favour as they, in their own opinion, deserved, they devoted themselves to the building and furnishing of their Prague residences — by way of protest, as it were.

This withdrawal from Vienna intensified in the early 18th century as a result of the international political situation. When Louis XIV of France deprived the Habsburg Empire of its leading position in Central Europe and the interests of the Vienna Government had to turn to the East and South, the importance of the Czech Lands decreased — except that they continued to bear the larger part of the country's taxes — and the disappointed and offended Bohemian nobility withdrew into their proud Prague isolation with the secret hope that this beautiful town would once again become the residence of a king. In this manner the Bohemian aristocracy saved and protected the artistic prestige of Prague to the detriment of which Vienna grew in Baroque style, having, until that time, been a less important provincial town.

Prague High Baroque

The intensification of building activity in Prague in the early 18th century, comparable only to the Gothic period, arose out of Mathey's Roman Classicism of the last quarter of the 17th century. But it took place chiefly under the influence of its counterpart, radical Roman Baroque, called also Illusionistic or Perspective Baroque. Its characteristic features were convex and concave wavy walls and the Guarini principles of

The statue of St Luitgarde on Charles Bridge, 1710, the first and culminating work of M. B. Braun in Prague

The portal of Clam-Gallas Palace in Husova street in the Old Town, the work of M. B. Braun, made c. 1714 according to a design by J. B. Fischer of Erlach. The illusionistic reliefs below the Atlantes represent the deeds of Hercules.

interlinked elipsoids, which gave the entire building, including the vaults, dramatic movement and left an impression of irrational, unreal space upon the spectator.

Its first, partial application was on the Church of St Ursula (sv. Voršila) on Národní street. The picturesque curving portal was built by Marc Antonio Canevale in 1702—1704. Full Radical Baroque was, for the first time, implemented on the façade of the Lesser Town Jesuit Church of St Nicholas and immediately in its most perfect form.

The wavy double façade was finished in 1710 by the architect Christoph Dientzenhofer, probably according to plans by the architect Giovanni Santini-Aichl. It introduces the spectator to a dynamic and, in view of its construction, incomprehensible space of a nave with side chapels and galleries above them, whose ceilings are illusionistically split up into a grandiose fresco glorifying the patron saint of the church, St Nicholas, the work of the Vienna painter Johann Lucas Kracker in 1761.

[159 The presbytery with the dome was the most important work of the chief creator of

Prague Baroque, Kilian Ignaz Dientzenhofer, Christoph's son; it was added in the second third of the 18th century, when the period of High Baroque was actually over in Prague.

The second Prague building of Radical Baroque was the monastery Church of St Margaret (sv. Markéta) at Břevnov, another work by Christoph Dientzenhofer in 1708—1714, based on a system of interlinked elipsoids. Its plastically modelled side aisle is adjacent to an ingeniously placed courtyard enclosed by Baroque outbuildings, standing on the site of a Romanesque monastery destroyed by the Hussites. The interior of the church makes an impression on the spectator with the flowing members of the architecture and the attractive unified style enhanced by outstanding paintings by Petr Brandl of 1716—1719 on all altars.

By the side of churches of illusionistic character the first High Baroque aristocratic palaces appeared in the early 18th century in Hradčany and the Lesser Town, which in the Baroque period became districts inhabited by the aristocracy.

On the slopes of the Hradčany spur, next to the Archbishop's Palace Giovanni Battista Alliprandi built an extensive palace for Count Václav Vojtěch of Sternberg in 1697 to

The Coronation Procession of Maria Theresa on the Old Town Square in 1743, detail of an etching according to a drawing by J. J. Dietzler

1708. Alliprandi was a leading Prague architect and disciple of the Vienna architect Domenico Martinelli. He was responsible for introducing High Baroque to Bohemia. He introduced certain new motifs of Vienna designers, which he applied in an original manner. Among others the central cylindrical projections from which the palace wings with curved façades emerge. Invisible from Hradčany Square, Sternberg Palace (Šternberský palác) surprises the visitor by the originality of its layout: it is not set on the square but has its axis towards the garden—artistically in an upward direction of the richly decorated walls of the inner courtyard.

The palace now houses the Collections of European Art of the National Gallery, including a remarkable Collection of Modern French Painting and Sculpture. There used to be a picture gallery here already at the beginning of the 19th century. At that time it was a private enterprise of a few noblemen who wished to raise the declining level of art in Bohemia, and it later became the basis of the official gallery, from which the present National Gallery in Prague was established.

Architect Giovanni B. Alliprandi enriched Prague with several more palaces at artistically very important places. In the Lesser Town he designed and built in 1703—1707 the imposing Palace of the Přehořovský family of Kvasejovice, which later came into the ownership of Count Kolowrat and, from 1753 on, the Lobkowicz family, whose name it bears to this day. It is now used as Embassy of the Federal Republic of Germany. This monumental building rises in Vlašská street and in sovereign manner dominates there as an effective counterweight to the mighty Schwarzenberg Palace at Hradčany. Its flexibly articulated garden façade with cut off wings and cylindrical projections in the centre is one of the most effective buildings of Prague Baroque, even though the addition of a further storey, carried out by the Lesser Town architect Ignatius Antonio Palliardi in 1769 somewhat spoilt the proportions of the original building.

The garden adjacent to the building is one of the largest in Baroque Prague. Originally it was an Italian terraced garden but was changed into an English park at the end of the 18th century and in 1800 the first rock garden in the city was laid out here. In 1740 the garden was one of the sights of the city greatly admired by foreign visitors.

Alliprandi contributed to the present appearance of the Lesser Town Square by rebuilding Sternberg Palace on its northern side incorporating in it the Renaissance House called "Bastion" where in 1541 the great fire broke out and where on the fateful day of 23rd May 1618 the Bohemian Estate met just before the defenestration. Alliprandi built Kaiserstein Palace whose dignified façade forms the artistic core of the entire eastern side of the square.

Giovanni Antonio Lurago, a Prague builder, made the plans for the reconstruction of Thun Palace in 1716—1727. Its double winged building of irregular ground plan is well hidden in Thunovská street in the Lesser Town at the foot of the New Castle Steps (Nové zámecké schody). The palace with its large terraced gardens below the Castle is today the British Embassy.

Alliprandi contributed in important manner to the Baroque reconstruction of the Old Town after a big fire in 1689, alleged to have been started by French incendiaries, during which several hundred houses burnt down. One of the main lines of communication in that part of the town, Celetná street, links the Old Town Square with the Powder Tower. Here Alliprandi designed the Palace of Count Hrzan of Harasov which far outshone the surrounding buildings in artistic quality.

Alliprandi proved his rare sense for the architectonic use of space when he made a project for a stone sculpture of the Holy Trinity on the upper Lesser Town Square in 1715. It was erected in gratitude for the disappearance of the plague from Prague. The tall obelisque rises from a sculptured base, made by Johann Udalrico Mayer and Ferdinand Geiger in front of the Jesuit College. It forms a perfect visual link between the centre of the Lesser Town and the Castle, which crowns the Square in the background.

[161

Two outstanding palaces show the rising cultural demands of the Bohemian aristocracy. They were designed by leading architects of Rome and Vienna. The Imperial Ambassador in Rome, J. Adam of Martinic, ordered plans for his palace in Loretánská street at Hradčany from Carlo Fontana, the famous architect of the post-Bernini period. The result is the only example in Prague of original, advanced contemporary Roman architecture. Johann Wenzel Gallas, Ambassador in Venice and London and Governor of Naples, turned to the famous Viennese architect Johann Bernhard Fischer of Erlach, from whom he commissioned a design for his Prague palace in Husova street in the Old Town.

Gallas (later Clam-Gallas) Palace was built in the years 1713—1729 and was magnificently adorned with sculptures from the workshop of Matthias B. Braun on the portal, attic, fountain and the staircase, which are some of the most beautiful in Prague.

The Astronomical Tower of the Clementinum with the leaden statue of Atlas Bearing the Armillary Sphere, 1721—1723, made according to a design by F. M. Kaňka, adapted by Anselmo Lurago in 1748

The palace represents a true jewel of Baroque architecture, since it perfectly combined the demands for public representation, comfortable living and highest artistic quality. Although wedged almost too tightly into the narrow medieval streets — the Count was unable to purchase the houses opposite — it was a great example for Prague Baroque architects, who adapted Viennese form to the local taste in original manner and at an exceptional level merged Roman Baroque with French Neo-Classicism.

The first to do so was a naturalized Italian architect Giovanni Santini-Aichl (1677—1723), who lived in Hradčany, one of the leading representatives of High Baroque in Bohemia. This creator of a new building style, Baroque Gothic, managed to merge, in ingenious manner, the Prague traditions in art as established by Mathey and Alliprandi with contemporary Roman stimuli (Borromini) and Viennese architecture (Fischer of Erlach, J. L. Hildebrand and J. Prandtauer).

The Library Hall of the Clementinum, 1727, according to a project by F. M. Kaňka, with allegorical ceiling paintings by J. Hiebl. Today it belongs to the State Library of the Czech Socialist Republic.

The effective contrast of expressively exaggerated architectonic sections and flat walls was adopted from him by architects of the following generation. His work was followed up by one of the most active of Bohemian architects of High Baroque, František Maxmilián Kaňka.

He designed two remarkable palaces in the present Nerudova street in the Lesser Town where he himself lived in Valkoun House in 1705, and two leading sculptors of Prague Baroque Ferdinand Maxmilian Brokoff and Matthias Bernard Braun provided the sculptural decorations.

Morzini Palace — now the Romanian Embassy — came into being in 1713—1714 when an Early Baroque house was rebuilt and joined up into one unit with other burghers' houses purchased for this purpose. The palace does not rise above the other houses, but smoothly fits among them. The restrained façade has few decorations in order to give stress to the sculpture. Two Brokoff Moors — the emblem of the Morzini family — hold up the balcony; lyrically conceived busts of Day and Night and allegorical figures of the Four Continents represent a perfect match of architecture and sculpture in Prague High Baroque style.

The palace opposite, Thun-Hohenstein Palace, is today the Italian Embassy. It was built in 1723—1726 for the Counts of Kolowrat. Its terse façade likewise forms a background to the outstanding sculptural decorations, this time from the workshop of M. Braun. There are two mighty pecking eagles on each side of the portal, the heraldic figures of the builder's family. The treble vestibule with columns and the stairway, re-

Self-Portrait of the sculptor F. M. Brokoff on the statue of St Francis Xavier on Charles Bridge, 1711. A copy of the original work has stood here since 1913.

A Turk Guarding the Imprisoned Christians on the statuary of SS John of Matha, Felix and Ivo on Charles Bridge, the work of F. M. Brokoff, 1714

newed in the eighties of the 19th century by artists of the Generation of the National Theatre (architect Josef Zítek, painters Josef Tulka and František Ženíšek), today recall the wealth and importance of the palace, which last century was the centre of artistic life in Prague.

In 1706—1707 the façade of the Church of Our Lady at the Theatins (Panny Marie U kajetánů) was built according to Santini's design near Theatin College above Thun-Hohenstein Palace. Santini took over the half-built church from the architect Mathey, as a plan for this church made by the leading Italian architect of Radical Baroque, Guarini, had not been implemented. He modelled the façade with a system of flat yet apparently plastic pillasters that stressed verticality in contrast with the horizontally laid out Thun-Hohenstein Palace, and created one of the first High Baroque churches in Prague.

Santini and Christoph Dientzenhofer were the founders of High Baroque. Their collaboration gave rise to the façade of St Nicholas' Church on the Lesser Town Square. And towards the end of his life Santini designed the dynamic western façade of the Town Church of St Gall, which was built after his death by P. J. Bayer.

One of the most active architects of Baroque Prague, who contributed to the establishment of the new style in Prague, was František Maxmilián Kaňka (1674—1766). He was the son of an Old Town builder and himself a citizen of the Old Town and collaborated with G. Alliprandi and G. Santini, from whom he learnt the basis of architecture. He managed to imprint upon adopted forms an original expression in which he balanced restrained simplicity with the charm of finely worked stucco decorations.

As architect of the Černín family he made additions to Černín Palace at Hradčany and built the second Černín Palace in Sněmovní street in the Lesser Town, which won him the approval of other noble families, for whom he designed and built palaces, châteaux and churches.

He was also a popular builder for the powerful Church Orders, mainly the Jesuits, for whom he projected and built the Church of St Clement, made additions to the Clementinum and on their recommendation reconstructed the Carolinum (1715—1718). Kaňka's skill was likewise used by the Augustinians in the Baroque reconstruction of the Gothic church of St Catherine (sv. Kateřina) — one of the most magnificent churches of Prague Baroque, its interior enhanced by ceiling frescoes by V. V. Reiner, and the adjacent monastery. He also built the prelature at Karlov.

For his aristocratic patrons he in turn built Pachta Palace in Celetná street in the Old Town (at the corner of Královorská street opposite the Old Mint), Lažan Palace in Sněmovní street and he also participated in the reconstruction of Oettingen Palace

The portal of Morzini Palace in Nerudova street in the Lesser Town by the architect J. Santini-Aichl with sculptural ornaments by F. M. Brokoff, 1714. The Moors supporting the balcony recall the heraldic motif of the palace builder, Count Morzini.

The portal of Thun-Hohenstein Palace in
Nerudova street in the Lesser Town by
J. Santini-Aichl with sculptural ornaments
by M. Braun, c. 1720

(opposite the Church of St Thomas in the Lesser Town) and Buquoy Palace, now the French Embassy on Grand Priory Square (Velkopřevorské náměstí).

For Count Jan Josef Vrtba, the Supreme Burgrave, Kaňka designed a Baroque garden using a dilapidated vineyard below the Petřín slope. In collaboration with his closest friends, sculptor M. Braun and painter V. V. Reiner, Kaňka created one of the artistically most attractive terraced Baroque gardens in Prague with a magnificent view over the town.

[167
Kaňka was the most successful Baroque architect in Prague, with the highest income,

and he owned seven houses and vineyards in the city. One of the most remarkable house in Národní street was designed by him, Kaňka House with a beautiful stucco façade; it got its name from one of the architect's descendants, the lawyer Kaňka, who was the owner.

In the second decade of the 18th century another native of Prague, Kilian Ignaz Dientzenhofer (1689—1751), worked by the side of Kaňka. He was born in the Lesser Town and was Christoph Dientzenhofer's son. In his work the period of Prague Baroque reached its climax and came to an end. A certain break occurred in the work of the younger Dientzenhofer, who lived into the second half of the 18th century, which foreshadowed the development of architecture and art in the subsequent period, when it was marked by the consequences of Habsburg absolutism, centralism and enlightened utilitarianism.

Kilian Ignaz Dientzenhofer received what was for his time an excellent education. He studied at the Lesser Town Jesuit grammar school and later attended lectures on philosophy and mathematics at Prague University. As a nineteen-year-old he was sent by his father on a study tour abroad, from which he returned nine years later. Apart from projects of his own he cooperated on his father's buildings and after the latter's death in 1722 undertook another study trip to Italy, France and perhaps England. This closed his early period, under Viennese influence, and then began the culminating period of his work, in which principles and motifs of radical Bohemian Baroque, as developed by his father and Giovanni Santini-Aichl, combined with the influence of Borromini and Guarini, to produce spatial phenomena of such creative freedom and originally as are typical only of the greatest artists. In the late period of his life K. I. Dientzenhofer followed European progress and turned towards French Neo-Classicism and Rococo.

Kilian Ignaz Dientzenhofer was one of those rare personalities who managed to imprint his seal not only on individual buildings but on the whole town. His first independent building in Prague, the summer palace of the Michnas of Vacínov, also colled Villa America, near St Catharine's Church in the New Town with a garden decorated with statues from the workshop of M. Braun, is one of the most charming pieces of Baroque architecture in Prague. It now houses the Antonín Dvořák Museum, as the composer lived in this part of town.

Each of Dientzenhofer's works dealt with an architectural problem in novel manner. The artist's inexhaustible imagination was a guarantee that he did not have to repeat himself. His first Prague church was St John's of Nepomuk (sv. Jan Nepomucký) at Hradčany, in 1720—1728; it was completed just before the solemn sanctification of the new Bohemian Baroque Saint, and before Prague Baroque reached its culmination here. He designed the church as a circular one with a grand fresco by V. V. Reiner representing the Legend of St John of Nepomuk on the vault of the church. The second church consecrated to the same saint (sv. Jan Nepomucký Na skalce — on the Rock) in Vyšehradská street opposite Emmaus Monastery was built in 1729—1739 in the spirit of perspective illusionistic Baroque on a ground plan of an elongated octagon.

The inner space is determined by the convex areas of the walls, alternatingly undulating and smooth. The windows of different shapes are located at different levels, giving rise to a multitude of new views which seem to draw together the vaulting into multi-shaped unity. Two richly modelled towers with laterns built obliquely in the church façade form the dominating features of the entire district and give the passers-by changing perspectives as they view the church that rises on a terrace above the sloping street.

K. I. Dientzenhofer set the tone in Prague architecture with his mature art from the twenties of the 18th century. He had studied the most advanced European patterns, and he did his work with a rare spatial imagination and great ease. In these two quali-

The America Summer House in Ke Karlovu street
in the New Town built to a plan by
K. I. Dientzenhofer for J. V. Michna of Vacínov,
1712—1720. Today the Antonín Dvořák Museum

ties he seemed to follow up the Later Gothic architect Benedikt Ried, with whom he was linked also in the function of builder of fortifications. Dientzenhofer became so famous in this field during the occupation of Prague in 1742 that two years later he was to be raised to the nobility. But he refused the honour, pointing out the difficult economic situation in which he found himself.

K. I. Dientzenhofer perfectly understood his native town and always underlined its great points. Each of his works grew directly out of the setting, the area of the street or square, and fitted sensitively into it in height, mass and harmonious modelling. The picturesque background of the Hradčany Loretto opposite Černín Palace—on which he collaborated with his father Christoph — enclosed this intimate Loretto Square (Loretánské náměstí). By rebuilding the burnt-down Church of St Thomas in the Lesser Town he imprinted dynamic Baroque form on this important sacral building ingeniously composed into the narrow space behind the Lesser Town Square. The façade of the church with the cascade of apparently mobile architectural elements is intentionally calculated to be seen from below.

In different manner he designed the façade and interior of the Church of St Charles Borromeo (sv. Karel Boromejský) in the New Town, which is today the Church of SS Cyril and Methodius of the Russian Orthodox Church. Quite different from this

The Prague Child Jesus, Spanish wax work
of the 16th century in the church of Our
Lady-Victorious in Karmelitská street,
a world-famous object of devotion

was St Nicholas' Church on the Old Town Square, in which a French type was adapted to the Prague setting. Dientzenhofer's own summer house in Smíchov, later called Buquoyka and Portheim Villa, which he built in 1725 for his family, is charming to this day for its playful architecture. His greatest and most important work, the completion of the Lesser Town Church of St Nicholas in the years 1737—1753, made a basic contribution, on a highly exposed site, to the entire panorama of the city.

It was a masterly stroke when he placed such a monumental dome and tower of St Nicholas' into the core of the western Prague basin. The upper part of the tower was completed by his son-in-law Anselmo Lurago. With this deed he gave final shape to the dominating feature of the Lesser Town, which harmoniously complements the silhouette of Hradčany. This church with its great solidity, collosal scale and important role in the image of Prague became a unique memorial to the creative genius of the two Dientzenhofers. The two famous architects lived in a house that they adapted for themselves in Nosticova street behind the Nostitz Riding School, and they are buried closeby in the Church of St Mary Magdalene in Karmelitská street (now the Central State Archives).

Prague — Baroque Town

Baroque changed the face and outline of the town in a more penetrating and thorough way than the Renaissance. The sharp points of the Gothic towers were replaced by rounded Baroque helms on the churches of SS James, Castulus and Gall, and the monasteries of Emmaus and Strahov were also adapted in Baroque. The number of towers increased and their domes and curves enriched the silhouette of Prague — the Astronomical Tower in the Clementinum, the towers of the Churches of St Saviour, St John-on-the-Rock, Our Lady-Victorious and others. New domes emerged above the town — at the Church of St Francis of the Knights of the Cross, St Saviour, St Nicholas in the Old Town, the tower at Karlov and, most important, St Nicholas in the Lesser Town, which did most to imprint upon Prague the image of a Baroque town.

While the architects adapted the churches, monasteries, aristocratic palaces and town houses in Baroque, the painters opened up views into heavenly paradise or ancient

The silver tomb of St John of Nepomuk in the southern ambulatory of St Vitus' Cathedral, the work of the Viennese goldsmith J. Würth, 1733—1736, according to a model by the sculptor A. Corradi and a sketch by the architect J. E. Fischer of Erlach

mythology on their illusive frescoes on the vaults of churches and ceilings of palaces. The sculptors enlivened portals, attics, niches, bridges, stairways and terraces with dynamic sculpture, adding corner figures and house signs to the sculpture of houses, stressing the area of a square with plague columns or nooks of streets with statues of St John of Nepomuk.

Prague Baroque is a good example of how all forms of art become interlinked aiming at creating a unified work of art, in which the borderline between individual branches vanished. Such a unified work took hold of the spectator and raised him to heavenly heights of miracles and religious visions or the legendary world of the gods and heroes of Antiquity. In Prague, architecture merged with sculpture more easily than elsewhere, painting became an illusion of space and sculpture lay close to painting.

The determining element that gave Baroque Prague such a unique character was plasticity with its roots in the natural prerequisites of the city. Since the architects of High Baroque paid regard to the relief of the Prague terrain in designing churches, palaces, gardens, summer houses, town streets and squares, the whole entity leaves a natural impression. It seems to us that the Prague Baroque architects and sculptors simply stressed and artistically enhanced the modelling of the land which was carved out by the Vltava in the prehistoric era.

How masterfully Prague Baroque managed to link its artistic aims with the given nature

View of the New World at Hradčany, a picturesque corner on the approach to the Hradčany district

can be shown in exemplary manner by the garden architecture on the slopes of Petřín Hill and below Prague Castle, which to this day give the town its greatest charm. Terraces, steps, ramps, garden houses, gloriettes, sala terrenas and grottoes were laid out with flower beds, shrubs and garden sculpture to form an intricate system, in which the architectonic elements skilfully and softly complement the natural features. Furthermore, the Prague Baroque gardens offer visitors unexpected and therefore the more attractive views of the city.

While Prague today surprises with its innumerable Baroque statues, it can pride itself of an exhibition under the open sky in the midst of the city; this is provided by Charles Bridge (Karlův most) with its sculptural decorations. The Angel Bridge in Rome is of earlier date, but the Prague bridge is richer, and its display more varied.

The oldest work on Charles Bridge is the Crucified Christ in the statuary of the Calvary on the site where a Cross stood already in the 14th century. The first statue was put up in 1683 in honour of St John of Nepomuk, whose body was cast into the river from the bridge. The bronze statue of this Czech Baroque Saint, according to a sketch by the Viennese sculptor Matthias Rauchmüller and a model by Johann Brokoff, was cast by Master J. W. Heroldt of Nuremberg.

In the period of High Baroque in the early 18th century, to be exact in the short period between 1707 and 1714, all other Baroque statues were put in the places where we can see them on the bridge to this day. They were commissioned by the most powerful representatives of contemporary political and cultural life, primarily the Jesuits, the aristocracy and the rich patricians.

The leading artists who made this gallery of sculpture, which taught Prague sculptors down to the second half of the 18th century, were the two representatives of Prague High Baroque sculpture: Ferdinand Maxmilian Brokoff and Matthias Bernard Braun. The first of these made eight works. The sculptor included his self-portrait in the face of the young man with the book in the statuary of St Francis Xavier. Among his works greatest attention is attracted by the group of Trinitarians with the popular figure of the fat Turk guarding the imprisoned Christians in a cave.

An outstanding work by Matthias Braun is the statue of St Luitgarde, the first and culminating work of this artist from the Tyrol, made soon after his arrival in Prague.

These two protagonists represent two currents in Czech Baroque sculpture. Alongside their works stand those of other Prague and foreign masters who are less well-known. Their sculptural élan, imbued with the emotional and sensual spirit of the time, distinguishes all Baroque statuary from 19th-century works, which replaced some of the older sculpture on the bridge pillars (Josef and Emanuel Max).

The local current of sculpture with its monumental realism found its highest expression in the work of Ferdinand Maxmilian Brokoff. This type of work had been carried out in the 17th century by Jan Jiří Bendl, the artist who made the first new era monument in Prague — an equestrian statue of St Wenceslas in stone, which originally stood in the middle of today's Wenceslas Square and can now be found at Vyšehrad. On the other hand, Braun's workshop enriched Prague with exciting works of radical Bernini illusionism.

Mystical visions of religious ecstacy and a hitherto unknown mighty surge of spirit roused by profound passions were embodied in rough-grained Bohemian sandstone with such conviction that it evoked the illusion of living shape and suggested vehement movement. Brokoff outdid his predecessors Ottavio Mosto (gable relief on the façade of the Church of St James in the Old Town — 1695) and Matthias Wenzel Jäckel (statues on St Francis' Church of the Knights of the Cross, the statues of the Virgin and St Bernard, the Virgin and SS Dominic and Thomas Aquinus and of St Anne on Charles Bridge) and in all spheres of sculptural work made such striking and effective types that Prague sculptors used them as inspiration still in the second half of the 18th century.

ČS STRANA LIDOVÁ
TABÁK
dorty
KAVÁRNA

View of the Dome of St Nicholas' Church on the Lesser Town Square built according to a project by K. I. Dientzenhofer, 1737—1752. The immense statues of the Church Fathers were carved by the sculptor I. F. Platzer in 1769.

◄
St Nicholas' Church on the Lesser Town Square, the most outstanding building of Radical Baroque in Prague. The work of Christoph Dientzenhofer, 1704—1711, the dome and apse were built by Kilian Ignaz Dientzenhofer 1737—1752 and the bell-tower added by Anselmo Lurago in 1755.

Prague Baroque painting was lucky to have as its leading personality in the forties of the 17th century a man of such greatness and importance as Karel Škréta Šotnovský of Záhořice. Born in Prague in an educated burgher's family, members of the Union of Brethren, he was raised to the rank of patrician. His uncle Daniel was one of the thirty leaders of the anti-Habsburg rising in 1618—1619 and went into exile with his family in 1627.

With him went his fellow students and artists, the Rudolphinian painters G. Sadeler and Václav Hollar, who later become the leading graphic artist of Baroque in England and was known and in demand all over Europe.

The Church of St John of Nepomuk-on-the-Rock in Vyšehradská street in the New Town, an outstanding illusionistic Baroque building by K. I. Dientzenhofer, 1730—1739. The stairway was added by the architect J. Schmidt, c. 1770.

176]

Interior of the Church of St Nicholas on the
Old Town Square, the work of
K. I. Dientzenhofer, 1732—1735

The Vision of St Hubert, house sign of the Burgher's House "At the Golden Stag" in Tomášská street, No. 26, in the Lesser Town, built by K. I. Dientzenhofer. The sculpture was made by F. M. Brokoff in 1726.

Karel Škréta spent five years in Italy, where he came to know all main centres of art. In Rome he became acquainted with the main representative of French Neo-Classicism, Nicolas Poussin. He became a Catholic and returned to Prague in 1638 to win back the confiscated family property. He went to court over this property against the authorities for thirty whole years and, on the whole, successfully, and during that time he became the leading painter of Prague in the period after the Battle of the White Mountain. In his work he linked stimuli from Italy, the Netherlands and Spanish Baroque with the local tradition and initiated an original local style, which was followed up by Prague High Baroque painters.

What Poussin menat for Paris, Rubens for Antwerp and Rembrandt for Amsterdam, Škréta represented for Prague. His dramatically effective altarpieces, especially in the Týn and Maltese Churches, and his magnificent realistic portraits — to be seen in the exhibition of Bohemian Baroque in St George's Convent — show the mastery with which he dealt with all contemporary problems of European painting and added his personal contribution.

In the first half of the 18th century the Prague High Baroque School of Painters is represented in the altarpieces of Petr Brandl (1668—1735) and frescoes by Václav Vavřinec Reiner (1689—1743). Both were born in Prague and did not need to go on study tours to Italy to acquire masterfulness and creative genius. At the time in Prague itself Baroque culture was strong and inspiring, and the picture galleries at the Castle and in the aristocratic palaces provided a setting full of all kind of stimuli, character and strength. This was aided by the presence of foreign painters — J. R. Bys of Switzerland, the Flemish artist A. Godyn, M. V. Halbax of Austria, the Silesian M. L. Willmann and his stepson J. K. Liška. At the very beginning of the High Baroque period, in 1709, architect F. M. Kaňka, sculptor F. Preiss and painter M. V. Halbax submitted a request for permission to set up an Academy of Fine Arts in Prague, but this idea was not realized for another ninety years.

The stairway of Grand Priory Palace in the Lesser Town was constructed by the architect Bartolomeo Scotti in 1726—1727. The scupltural decorations come from the workshop of M. B. Braun.

Kolowrat Garden, the most beautiful of the Lesser Town gardens below Prague Castle, designed by the architect Ignaz Palliardi, c. 1785

In the Baroque period Prague became a treasure house of art, both in a literal and a figurative sense. Works of sculpture, painting and decorative arts filled monasteries, churches, aristocratic summer palaces and burghers' houses, safe behind the tall ring of Baroque fortifications. Every more important church could pride itself upon magnificent monstrances, chalices, reliquaries of gold, silver and precious stones, and today we can see such works in the St Vitus Treasure and in the Loretto Treasure.

One's imagination barely suffices to vizualize the magnificent interiors of buildings belonging to the secular and ecclesiastic aristocracy. Such original furnishings are still to be found in the Archbishop's Palace at Hradčany. There were precious tapestries from Brussels or Paris, Venetian mirrors, inlaid furniture — supplied to the monasteries and palaces by the Prague carpenter Jan Drobner — carved goblets, cut and double-walled glasses and crystal glass chandeliers from local Bohemian glasshouses. And so we can understand that Prague, in the Baroque period, lived through one of the most magnificent and most stimulating periods of its history, in which all possibilities of art were applied in building a beautiful city, where construction work took full and sensitive advantage of the relief of the undulating Prague territory.

Rococo and Neo-Classicism

High Baroque in Prague was reaching its end when Emperor Charles VI (1711—1740) died in Vienna. He was the younger brother of the prematurely deceased Joseph I (1705—1711). Since Charles VI had no son, only daughters, and out of fear that the Habsburg Monarchy might disintegrate after his death into individual and independent countries, he published the Pragmatic Sanctions in 1713, according to which the countries ruled by the Austrian Habsburgs — the Kingdoms of Bohemia and Hungary, and the Austrian Dukedom — were to form one inseparable enclave, and hereditary rights were to be handed down on the paternal and maternal side. Ferdinand I embodied this law into the new Constitution of Bohemia in 1627, being most concerned with Hungary where the inheritance of the Habsburg kings referred only to the male line.

View of Nerudova street in the Lesser Town, originally the main road leading to Prague Castle, named after the poet Jan Neruda, who lived in the Baroque House "At the Two Suns" (No. 233)

Even though the Pragmatic Sanctions were acknowledged by all countries of the Habsburg Monarchy and the main European powers, as soon as the young Maria Theresa ascended the throne after her father's death, France and Bavaria, Saxony and Prussia disregarded them. This war over the Bohemian inheritance of the young but energetic Queen deprived the state of Bohemia of Silesia, the most highly industrialized and most densely populated land of the Bohemian Crown. Maria Theresa, in the end, defended her throne, but Prague was bombarded several times during the war, was conquered and looted, and the people of Prague had to pay high contributions to the French and the Prussians. And during the siege of Prague by the Prussian soldiers in 1757 artillery shelling destroyed or badly damaged about one third of all Prague houses, and even Prague Castle was partly ruined.

The onset of the reign of Maria Theresa affected the Czech Lands and Prague in other ways, too. When the foreign armies at the end of 1741 conquered the town, and the Elector of Bavaria, Charles Albert, was proclaimed King of Bohemia, most of the Bohemian nobles paid homage to him in Vladislav Hall. Since a year later Prague was occupied by the Habsburg army, the Bohemian noblemen had to submit a petition of pardon to the Queen, who granted it magnanimously, so that in the spring of 1743 the solemn coronation of Maria Theresa as Queen of Bohemia took place in St Vitus' Cathedral. The embarassing episode with Charles Albert did not help to increase the Vienna Government's sympathy for the Czech and for Prague, which waited in vain to become once again a monarch's summer residential town.

The war affected the surroundings of Prague outside the Baroque fortifications in decisive manner. The vineyards disappeared almost completely, so did hop-gardens and orchards, which had formed a green belt around the town since the Gothic period, separating it from its agricultural hinterland. These areas were now occupied by large estates and houses of the nobility used as summer residences.

With the rule of Maria Theresa, from the forties of the 18th century on, there came changes in Prague architecture and in the other arts, and new styles began to appear, which are generally known as Rococo and Neo-Classicism. Their homeland was the France of Louis XV, and most of them reached Prague via imperial Vienna. They left a mark on the last buildings by K. I. Dientzenhofer, Piccolomini's Palace on Příkopy street (1743—1751) — later called Sylva-Taroucca Palace, today the Club of Education and Science — and Golz-Kinský Palace on the Old Town Square (1755—1765); Dientzenhofer's plans for this were implemented by his son-in-law Anselmo Lurago. The basically Neo-Classical palace has rich stuccowork of plastic roses and French rocaille on the façade with a playful rhythm of Rococo, and this makes it one of the most beautiful examples of this style in Prague. A. Lurago probably also participated in building the Rococo Caretto-Millesimo Palace in Celetná street.

Most of the building construction in Theresan Prague was undertaken or stimulated by the ruler herself, who started major reconstruction at Prague Castle in the years 1753—1755, during which new parts were added. It is irony of fate that the Baroque changes of the basically Gothic town were undertaken by the Empress who, through legal reforms aimed at modernizing the monarchy and ensuring its coherence, condemned Prague to the role of a provincial town.

The reconstruction was supervised by the imperial Viennese architect Nicolo Pacassi, who made the overall design and left the detailed execution to Prague architects and builders. Sculptural decorations were provided by the leading Prague master Ignaz Franz Platzer and his workshop. His contemporary Norbert Grund, the leading painter of Prague Rococo, made a painting of him while busy at work on a statue for Prague Castle. The reconstruction of the Castle began with the Institute of Noblewomen, for which the former Rožmberk Palace opposite the Church of St George was adapted, and extended to the entire entrance wing and the side overlooking the town.

At that time Prague Castle finally lost its medieval character. The moats to the west were filled in and formed today's first courtyard — the *cour d'honneur* approached from Hradčany Square — and the second courtyard where a unified appearance was given to older buildings. In 1756 Anselmo Lurago designed and built the Holy Rood Chapel. The continuous, slightly curving southern front of the Castle underlined the Hradčany panorama with its colossal, though slightly monotonous horizontal line, out of which rise only the Neo-Gothic towers of St Vitus' Cathedral, built in the 20th century. The architecture of the façades showed a certain schematism and economical restraint as the result of enlightened utilitarianism and lack of funds. For the state treasury was constantly at low ebb in consequence of the continuous long wars.

These Viennese Neo-Classical and Rococo elements — mainly found in the interior furnishings of the Castle palaces — tempted Prague to follow suit. But Dientzenhofer's example did find some echo in the second half of the 18th century too. Except that instead of the aristocracy, responsible for building activity in High Baroque, the role was now taken over by the burghers of Prague, particularly those who had been awarded coats-of-arms.

The patriciate raised to the nobility took the place of the aristocracy at the very time

Bertramka Villa in Smíchov, a Baroque homestead from the 17th century, made famous by W. A. Mozart, who stayed here in the years 1787 and 1791. Today the Mozart Museum

when the latter, as a consequence of Theresan reforms which attracted the aristocrats to Vienna, post-war economic problems and the decline of agricultural production, had lost interest in building and maintaining representative palaces in Prague. The burghers with a noble title and grown rich as army purveyors and from investment in industry followed up aristocratic Baroque, but their palaces fit the better into the streets and blend into the simpler burghers' houses rebuilt after war damage in 1757. At that time the street fronts become a picturesque and continuous setting, modelled and given rhythm by the movement of light and shade.

Three architects grew out of the tradition of Prague High Baroque and applied the new Rococo approach on their palaces. Jan Josef Wirch of the New Town designed in Rococo style the Archbishop's Palace at Hradčany, built the Mint with a balcony held up by the statues of miners and soldiers made in I. F. Platzer's workshop, and Pachta Palace in Karolíny Světlé street, whose charming Rococo architecture is hidden in the courtyard of Empire blocks of apartment houses.

The Lesser Town became the home of Josef Jäger of the Tyrol, who built the large, originally Renaissance Smiřický Palace on Maltese Square in simple manner for the nouveau-rich John of Montague, who had been raised to the nobility. On the same square he built Turba Palace — now the Japanese Embassy — whose façade, adorned with striking Rococo decoration, contrast with the simple façade of the house opposite, which this architect and builder adapted for himself.

The Lesser Town architect Anton Schmidt did not abandon the Dientzenhofer example even in the seventies, as shown by Kounic Palace in Mostecká street in the Lesser Town, although antique elements did appear on the decorations of the façade. An example of the increasing artistic demands of the Prague citizens is Kučera Palace at Pohořelec, built in 1775—1780 for the rich family of chimney-sweep Demartini. Its charmingly adorned façade is one of the most attractive buildings of Prague patriciate Rococo.

The two wars which Maria Theresa had to wage in defence of the Habsburg Monarchy revealed all the shortcomings of the reactionary empire. The reforms she by degrees introduced were to modernize the monarchy in all spheres of internal life and thereby strengthen its international standing. The leading principle of these reforms was centralization and its consequence, or method of application, which affected the Czech Lands so badly, was Germanization.

The Bohemian state of the Estates, as set up by Ferdinand II in the new Constitution of 1627, was, in fact, changed into a mere province administered by state officials; this intensified in 1749, when the Empress — in contradiction to her vows at the coronation — abolished the separate Bohemian Office in Vienna and merged it with the Austrian Office.

This interference in the traditional privileges of the Bohemian nobility strengthened local patriotism and stirred endeavours to protect the historical rights of Bohemia. The Germanization roused national consciousness among the intellectuals which stimulated the awakening Revival Movement. This Germanization was not a deliberate measure and was not turned against the Czechs with bad intentions. Its aim was simply to even out the considerable differences in national groups and to ease the work of the state administration. The removal of Czechs from offices, authorities, schools, literature, public and social life caused a reaction among the Czech patriots, who changed the slogan of the Age of Enlightenment from "All for the State" to "All for the Nation" and with youthful élan and courage began to propagate it.

The nationality question sharpened when Maria Theresa was followed on the throne by her son, the ruthless reformer Emperor Joseph II (1780—1790), who introduced decrees to change his feudal state into an absolutist one, organized on the principle of enlightened reason. In 1781 he abolished serfdom and proclaimed freedom of religion for the Protestants and the Orthodox Church; in 1784 he abolished the last remains of

V. V. Reiner, The Last Judgment, grandiose ceiling fresco in the dome of the Church of the Knights of the Cross in the Old Town, 1722—1723

the medieval administration of Prague, removed the outdated institution of the Royal Judges and placed a magistrate with trained clerks at the head of the city.

Hradčany had been the last to be raised to the status of royal town in 1592; in 1657 together with the Lesser Town it gained the same status as the Old and the New Town. Under Joseph II all the Towns of Prague were merged into one community administered by one single Municipal Council, and all former autonomous authorities were abolished. The result was that the clerks of the Municipal Council worked in more qualified manner than the elected counsellors, but any direct influence exerted by the citizens of Prague on the administration of their town was out of the question.

On the one hand, Emperor Joseph II, true to his principles of Enlightenment, supported the establishment of social, medical and charitable institutions. A general hospital was founded in Prague at that time (on today's Charles Square), a maternity hospital, an orphanage and alms houses. On the other hand, he abolished with unheard-of radicalism all Catholic churches and monasteries. During the reign of Maria Theresa, when Joseph had been co-regent, the Jesuit Order was dissolved, and its property was taken over by the government. In 1782 the Emperor then proceeded to liquidate all churches and monastery buildings that had no important, socially advantageous purpose. Prague lost twenty-three monasteries and thirty-five churches and chapels, which were either demolished or adapted for other purposes.

Ten monasteries were turned into barracks. No cultural or historical regards were respected. The only criterion was usefulness. Among the various demolished churches was also the Bethlehem Chapel, all the three known and still standing rotundas from the Romanesque period, and even the oldest convent in Bohemia, St George's at Prague Castle, including its convent church. The property of the disolved ecclesiastical

Karel Škréta, detail from the picture Portrait of the Gem-Cutter Dionysio Miseroni and his Family, probably 1653. National Gallery, Prague

Petr Brandl, Simeon and the Christchild, after 1725, masterly example of the artist's mature work and his temperamental brushwork. National Gallery, Prague

The grandiose ceiling fresco by the Viennese painter A. Maulbertsch, 1794, in the Philosophical Hall of the Strahov Library, depicts the History of Mankind.

institutions fell to the state and their valuable furnishings, including precious libraries, were sold at ridiculously low prices.

The Germanization of Prague reached its peak at the time of Joseph, and from 1784 on all lectures at the university had to be given solely in German. The town, which had retained its Bohemian character until the middle of the 18th century, began to change even in language under the influence of the Theresan administrative reforms. The nobility spoke and felt German, and the wealthier town people copied them. Only the new rural people, now free from serfdom, who moved into the town, brought along their pithy spoken Czech and thus fortified the city divided by nationality. Yet in that city, which in the last decade of the 18th century was given an external German veneer, there grew up the centre of the Revival Movement under the Romantic slogan of Czech patriotism, and in the end showed itself capable of overcoming even the most dangerous Josephinian Germanization.

The Josephinian reforms put an end to the enterprise of the Church and nobility so that there cannot be found many representative Neo-Classical buildings from the eighties of the 18th century. The most important is the building of the Strahov Library with a façade adorned with vases and symbolic attributes and medallion of Emperor Joseph II by sculptor Ignaz Platzer the Younger.

The designer of the Library Ignaz Anton Palliardi, of the Lesser Town, also built Kolowrat Palace and reconstructed Ledebour Palace in Valdštejnská street, with a terraced Baroque garden behind both palaces below the Castle, which is among the most beautiful in the town. Further he made MacNeven Palace in Palackého street in the New Town, where in the 19th century there lived and died the greatest Czech historian and political leader František Palacký, the "Father of the Nation". In contrast with the strict Neo-Classicism of the Strahov Library, Palliardi's palaces have more of a traditional Baroque character.

Neo-Classicism also marked a monumental Prague theatre, which stands to this day, the Tyl Theatre (originally the Nostitz Theatre) in the Old Town, which was built out of funds provided by Count Nostitz-Reinecke in the years 1781—1783 by the architect Anton Haffenecker of the Lesser Town. He also adapted Nostitz Palace on Maltese Square and built a riding school in its garden.

The Nostitz Theatre was bought by the Czech Estates in 1798 and renamed the Estates Theatre. It was there that the world's first performance of Mozart's *Don Giovanni* took place on 29 October 1787. Mozart wrote this opera for his Prague audience, since they had received his music with such clear enthusiasm. Mozart wrote the opera that very year when he was the guest of the Dušek family — pianist František Xaver and his wife, the famous singer Josephine — and he stayed at their charming Baroque Bertramka Villa in Smíchov. Mozart had visited here in 1786 and came once again in 1791 on the occasion of the coronation of Leopold II, for which he composed a new opera *La Clemenza di Tito.* The interior of Bertramka Villa is now the Mozart Museum, and to this day there stands the piano on which the master used to play. In 1787 Mozart also stayed at the Dušek's house in the Old Town at the corner of the Coal Market and Skořepka street, where a memorial plaque was appended with a portrait head of the composer in 1956.

It was no mere chance that W. A. Mozart found such understanding and acknowledgement in Prague as nowhere else in Europe. Vienna had received his music rather coolly. In the second half of the 18th century, when the great and creative epoch of Prague Baroque was drawing to its end, the building programme exhausted and the material and ideological stimuli had died away as a consequence of wars and enlightened reforms, the Bohemian nobility in their palaces occupied themselves with historical studies and natural sciences and devoted a good deal of time to music. This assumed a leading role in Prague of the Enlightenment while the fine arts had been dominant in the Baroque period.

This is confirmed by a contemporary foreign observer, the English music historian Charley Burney, who regarded Prague as the most musical town in Europe. Its importance lay in it being a leading centre of musical pre-Classicism, which grew out of the local music tradition under the influence of Italian melodiousness at St Vitus' Cathedral where its main representative, František Xaver Brixi (1732—1771), was choirmaster.

Prague musicians of the pre-Classical current were also to be found in Mannheim, where Mozart's predeccessor in symphonic music, Jan Stamic, was working, in Vienna (Jan Václav H. Voříšek), in Paris (Antonín Rejcha) and obviously also in Italy, where Josef Mysliveček (1737—1781) was given the title "il divino Boemo".

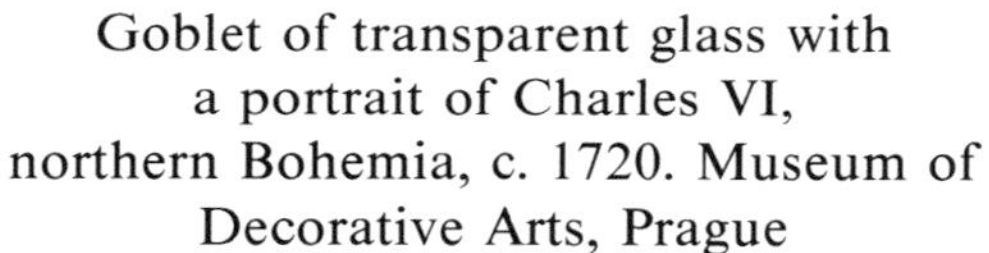

Goblet of transparent glass with a portrait of Charles VI, northern Bohemia, c. 1720. Museum of Decorative Arts, Prague

Czech Baroque goblet, double-walled, 1730—1740, with engraving of St Leopold in gold. Museum of Decorative Arts, Prague

Josephinian Enlightenment did not do much good to the fine arts. In 1782 all the remnants of the Rudolphinian Collections were sold at a public auction at ridiculous prices of a few coins. But it did stimulate scientific interests. The Royal Society of Bohemia was founded in 1784 and was one of the first scientific institutions in the Habsburg Monarchy. The foundations of scientific history studies were laid by the Piarist Gelasius Dobner (1719—1790), a monk of German origin, whose interest in the past history of Bohemia was so great that in his thinking he turned Czech.

National consciousness was effectively supported by František Martin Pelcl (1734—1801), the first professor of Czech Language and Literature at Prague University after 1793 and the author of a survey of Czech history. The true genius of the Generation of the Enlightenment was the ex-Jesuit Josef Dobrovský (1753—1829), world-famous founder of scientific Slavonic and Bohemian Studies, who educated the leading scientists of the Romantic generation in a critical spirit. This generation broadened the movement of the National Revival in the 19th century, giving it greater rhythm and stronger resonance.

The Burghers' City

Empire window of the House, today House
"At the Ibernians", 1808—1811

Empire Prague

Prague entered the 19th century in one of the most difficult and complicated periods of its history, the time of the Napoleonic Wars, stagnation of population and economic decline, which put a stop to artistic work and larger building enterprise.

In 1791 the town witnessed the ostentatious magnificence of the coronation festivities of Leopold II (1780—1892), Emperor Joseph II's younger brother, who was crowned King of Bohemia in St Vitus' Cathedral. But the town people's naive hope that the city might once again become a royal residence was soon dispelled. In 1794 the Viennese painter Anton Franz Maulbertsch made dazzling illusionistic paintings on the ceiling of the Philosophical Hall of the Strahov Library depicting the History of Mankind. The fragile figures, in their Rococo grace, float in a medium of light and colour and represent a slightly protracted final dot at the end of the grand chapter of Prague Baroque.

The situation in the fine arts in Prague, at the end of the 18th century, was so pitiful that the Bohemian nobility considered it their moral duty to see to improvements. In 1796 they established a private Society of Patriotic Friends of the Arts, which endeavoured to set up a picture gallery that same year, followed by the Academy of Fine Arts in 1800. This Prague Academy was only concerned with drawing in the first period and later became the axis of modern Czech painting as such, although few of the directors were leading artists themselves. Here all outstanding Czech painters and sculptors un-

The Tyl Theatre in the Old Town, built in 1781—1783 according to a plan by the architect A. Haffenecker and Count S. Künigel

The Coronation Procession of Emperor Leopold II
in 1791 on the Old Town Square, detail of an etching
by Kaspar Pluth, made in 1791 according to a drawing
by Philipp and Franz Heger

derwent their training, even if in their work they fought against or protested against the Academy's backward views on art and outdated teaching methods.

The Napoleonic Wars did not affect Prague directly. The people of Prague only felt the economic consequences, which, in 1811, lead to the state going bankrupt and the devaluation of the currency. Shortly before the outbreak of the war with revolutionary France in 1791 an Industrial Exhibition was held in the Clementinum, the first of its kind in Europe, and it rendered proof of the advanced condition of Bohemian manufactured products. At that time there existed the manufacture of printed cotton in the villages outside the city walls, mainly in Smíchov. Industry continued to develop in the vicinity of Prague, despite the difficulties of the wars, and it benefited from the Napoleonic continental blockade.

Soon after the end of the Napoleonic Wars in 1817 a new district, Karlín, was planned and laid out to become Prague's first proper suburb. It received its name from Empress Carolina Augusta, the wife of the Austrian Emperor Franz I (1792—1835). The new settlement lay in the area limited to the north by the River Vltava, to the south by the slopes of Vítkov Hill, and on the east by the Baroque building of the Invalid Soldiers' Home (Invalidovna), built by K. I. Dientzenhofer in 1731—1737. The remaining building is only a fragment of the original grandiose plan. From the 13th century on this place had been called "Hospital Fields" after the owners, the Hospitallers of the Convent of the Blessed Agnes, as the Knights of the Cross with a Red Star were called. In 1420 the famous Battle of Vítkov had taken place here in which the Hussites

The former Governor's Summer Palace in Stromovka Park founded by Vladislav of Jagiello at the end of the 15th century, re-built in Renaissance style by Emperor Rudolph II and changed into Neo-Gothic by the architect Georg Fischer in 1804. Today the Department of Journal of the Library of the National Museum

defeated the Emperor Sigismund for the first time. And it was here that the festive royal processions formed ranks before coronations in St Vitus' Cathedral.

In the Josephine period the Prague publisher Ferdinand Schönfeld built a summer house (called Růžodol) here with a tavern and a dance-hall set in a charming garden, its area symbolical of the map of Bohemia. After the Schönfelds left Prague in the early 19th century, the garden was built up with factories and dwelling houses to become a new district. Karlín was built on order of the Land Government, following a strict town plan with a regular chessboard layout, where three main lines of communication formed the axes and the centre lay in the midst of a big square that covered the entire width of the district. Here, to this day, stands the parish Church of SS Cyril and Methodius in one of the oldest of Prague parks, and it is one of the most important pieces of architecture in the district.

Built in 1854—1863 according to a design by the Viennese architect Karel Rössner and the Prague architect Ignaz Ullmann, it represents the first church architecture in Prague in the period of Historicism (Eclecticism). The church has the proportions of the balanced Romanesque basilica with a transept and two towers on the entrance side, and leading Czech artists took part in the decorations. The painter Josef Mánes designed the reliefs on the bronze door and painted the picture of the Patron Saints of

Bohemia on a side altar. The sculptor Václav Levý carved the three tympanons on the façade.

Karlín is the industrial district of Prague, in the thirties of the 19th century one of the largest plants producing steam engines for the Austrian Monarchy was opened here, and in 1847 the first Prague gasworks began operation. In 1903 the district was raised to the status of town. Even though it was considerably modernized in the 20th century it retains to this day the character of an Empire town.

By contrast to Karlín, built to a regular plan, the building up of industrial Smíchov took place in an entirely unorganized manner. This Prague suburb on the left bank of the R. Vltava, south of the Lesser Town, had natural beauty already in the Middle Ages; there were flowering gardens, orchards and dense vineyards everywhere. In the Baroque period the vineyards were replaced by homes belonging to the upper classes surrounded by gardens, and a few of these — Buquoyka, Klamovka and Mozart's Bertramka — have survived. The wars during the reign of Maria Theresa laid waste the whole district, but its natural charm was soon renewed. However, the industrial development of the Empire period meant the beginning of the end of idyllically beautiful Smíchov.

To start with, the factories and dwelling houses kept to the main lines of communication — from time immemorial routes led south to Zbraslav and west to Plzeň — but later

The former Customs House on the Republic Square in the New Town, rebuilt in Empire style in 1808—1811 according to a plan by Georg Fischer from a dissolved Early Baroque Monastery Church of the Irish Franciscans (the Ibernians). Today the House of Exhibition Services

the entire landscape began to be built up. In only a few places did small gardens remain as the last reminders of the former beauty of Smíchov. Like Karlín Smíchov acquired town status in 1903.

The Empire period enriched Prague with fresh greenery to be found in the gardens inside blocks of buildings and along avenues, and in orchards along the edge of the town, on the islands in the river and the hill slopes rising out of the Vltava Basin. And during the Empire period the nobility and richer burghers began to lay out homesteads and summer houses surrounded with orchards and parks. Klamovka, on the edge of Smíchov and Košíře, stands in an English park with garden houses, a little temple of Night and curious monuments (1790—1820). Cibulka at Košíře was founded in 1817 by the Bishop of Passau, Prince Leopold Thun-Hohenstein, and is one of the most charming places in the Prague environs.

Nature, in the form of parks and avenues of trees, also made its presence felt in the inner town and along the walls. This was encouraged by the pre-Romanticism of the second half of the 18th century. Squares and streets were planted with trees, which improved the atmosphere. Avenues of lindentrees grew up on the filled-in moats between the Old and the New Town, in today's streets Na příkopě (after 1760) and Národní (1788), and they covered Charles Square in the very centre of the town.

The whole of the Prague environs changed into one continuous English park in the Late Empire or Biedermeier period (1820—1840). Petřín Hill was de-forested, and the Viennese architect Heinrich Koch built an attractive Empire villa for Count Rudolf Kinský there in 1827. Today this houses the Ethnographic Collections of the National Museum. The park on Štvanice Island attracted people on their Sunday promenades

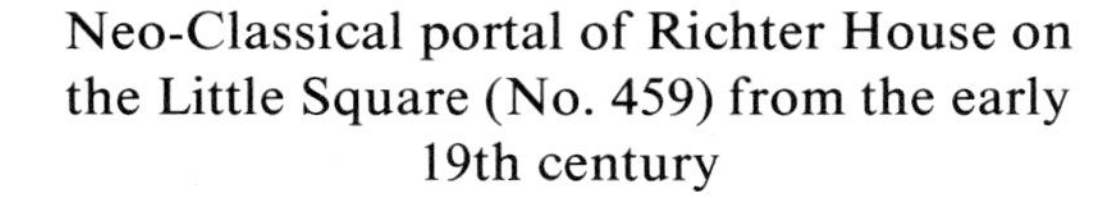

Neo-Classical portal of Richter House on the Little Square (No. 459) from the early 19th century

as did the gardens of today's Vinohrady, which were open to the public. The Royal Deer Park was changed in 1804 into the popular Stromovka Park. Chotek Park (laid out 1833) also became a public park. It derived its name from the founder, the Supreme Burgrave Karel Chotek.

The idyllic character of Empire Prague, surrounded by fresh green vegetation, was depicted on coloured etchings by Prague artists, led by the first Professor of Landscape Painting at the Prague Academy, Karel Postl.

It was typical of the slightly alien character of Prague Empire architecture, incorporating a large element of Romanticism, that all three main buildings were designed by the leader of the Construction Department of the Land Government, the Viennese architect Georg Fischer. He selected the style of English Romantic Gothicism in reconstructing the summer house in the Royal Deer Park (1804) belonging to the Governor (Místodržitelský letohrádek). In his plan for the building of the Customs House (now House of Exhibitions) on the site of the dissolved Monastery Church of the Ibernians (kostel hybernů), opposite the Powder Tower, he made use of the pattern of Gentz's Empire Old Mint in Berlin (1808), and he built the Church of the Holy Rood (sv. Kříž) on Na Příkopě street in strict Empire style (1816—1824).

Prague acquired its first apartment building in Národní street which to this day is called Plateys (Platýz) after the owner of the time, Johann Plateys of Plattenstein, who had it built in the Late Renaissance period. The Empire appearance of the once most expensive apartment house in Prague was the work of the architect Heinrich Hausknecht (1817—1825). It was said that the owner, Jakob Wimmer, earned a ducate every hour for renting out apartments.

Plateys Court on Národní street, one of the first apartment blocks in Prague, Empire reconstruction of a Renaissance Palace of Plateys of Plattenstein by the architect J. Hausknecht, 1817—1825

Neo-Classical façade of the House "At the Black Stag", No. 265, on the Lesser Town Square from the period after 1778, when its owner, Ignaz Palliardi, reconstructed it

Neo-Classical windows on House No. 262 on the Lesser Town Square designed by the architect I. Palliardi, end of the 18th century

Empire sculpture, mostly on the level of simple craftsmanship, concentrated on tombstones for lack of other commissions. The Lesser Town cemetery was laid out during the plague in 1680, and became the public cemetery of the Lesser Town and Hradčany in 1786 when Joseph II prohibited burial in the midst of the town. The cemetery became a gallery of Prague sculpture in the first half of the 19th century. Neo-Classical allegorical figures imbued with Romantic sentimentality are typical motifs of many cementery tombstones.

The work of sculptor Václav Prachner rose above this level, and his monumental tombstone of the kneeling Bishop of Passau, Leopold, Count Thun-Hohenstein, cast in iron in the Hořice Iron-Works in 1830—1831, influenced Myslbek's bronze statue of Cardinal, Friedrich, Count Schwarzenberg in St Vitus' Cathedral (1892—1895). V. Prachner also made one of the few public statues, an allegory of the Vltava — called Theresa by the people of Prague — which stands on Dr. Vacek Square.

Another remarkable civic sculpture, a charming fountain on the Coal Market, stood originally on Národní street. It was made by the sculptor František Xaver Lederer in 1797.

Painting provided more of interest in the first half of the 19th century. It was the time of the founding generation of artist, headed by the leading portraitist of the Czech Revivalist Society, Antonín Machek (1755—1844), the Revivalist Romanticist František Hořčička (1776—1856), the Romantic and Realist landscape painter Antonín Mánes (1784—1843), the figure painter and outstanding draughtsman František Tkadlík (1786—1840). The work of these painters opened the way for the classical artists of Czech painting, who, in the forties of the 19th century, were able to follow up and establish the new era tradition in national painting.

Romanticism and the National Revival

By contrast to other nations living under more favourable conditions, the Czechs had to overcome great difficulties and obstacles on the road to constituting the nation. They had to overpower such great opposition that it must have seemed a miracle to contemporaries that they did not succumb in this struggle. In the first place, they did not have their own state, and, as the consequence of lack of political freedom, they did not even form all the social classes and strata of their nation. They were opposed by the Habsburg Monarchy, which felt threatened by the national movement. They were oppressed by the might of Germany in political and economic life and threatening Germanization imposed by the government in Vienna. Furthermore, they could not rely on the support of the Bohemian nobility, who, in education, cultural orientation and marriages, had become alienated from their nation, and there was no rich patriciate that might take the place of the nobility in this regard.

When the tradition of Baroque local patriotism heightened interest in language, and the influence of romantic philosophy turned this into modern nationalism, the nobility ceased to show any interest in the nation. The leading role of the Czech Revival

The Lesser Town Square on Langweil's Model of Prague made in 1826—1834. Museum of the City of Prague

Wenceslas Square, once the Horse Market in the New Town, c. 1830, depicted on a veduta by V. Morstadt

Movement was played by modern Czech townspeople; and it was taken up by the patriotic intelligentsia, who came from the middle and lower classes.

This specific structure of the Czech nation explains why its National Revival Movement followed predominantly democratic and liberal aims. In the first period the success of the Revival Movement was due to the intellectuals, enthusiastic Revivalists, teachers, priests, writers, scientists and artists, but the largest and decisive merit in the ultimate victory was that of the Czech people, who never ceased to speak in their own language, and whose traditional culture of literature, music and art served as a well of inspiration for modern Czech artists.

The patriotic Bohemian nobility aimed at raising the material and cultural standards of the country in a generally progressive sense without any relationship to the National Revival Movement, and they, therefore, supported the activity of various Prague societies for the enhancement of the economy, the sciences and arts.

This led to the establishment of a Picture Gallery, the Academy and a Botanical Garden at Smíchov (1775), which existed until 1902. It used to lie close to Dientzenhofer Park-Square today. In 1806 a Polytechnical Institute was established, followed, in 1816, by the Conservatoire of Music. While in 1818 the nobility contributed to the foundation of the National Museum in Prague, and in 1833 helped to set up the Association for the Stimulation of Industry, they did not participate, in 1830, in the preparatory work for the setting up of the Czech Publishers, a branch of the Museum Association concerned with the publication of Czech scientific literature.

The moving forces behind the National Revival Movement involved Czech books and close links to the Czech theatre and the newspapers. When Václav Matěj Kramerius in 1789 began to publish the Imperial and Royal Post Paper in the house "At the

Golden Half-Wheel" (U zlatého půlkola) in Michalská street No. 23, he turned to the common people in Prague and in the countryside, since they were his only subscribers. And the Patriotic Czech Theatre, in a provisional wooden building called The Shed on Wenceslas Square, played an exclusively popular repertory in 1786—1789 since the majority of spectators were small craftsmen and workers.

At the very beginning of the 19th century the very term "Czech" meant a poor, propertyless man. An article by Josef Jungmann in 1828 shows that the situation did not change much in the next quarter of a century, but that the need for change was acutely felt. Jungmann speaks of support for the Czech nation in raising their economic potential. For a poor nation can hardly undertake economic activity or create culture or works of art. The Czech Savings Bank, the first credit institution in Prague, was founded in 1825, but it took two decades before Czech burghers took their place by the side of English, French, German and Austrian industrial entrepreneurs.

The Czech middle classes, which formed in the forties of the 19th century on the eve of the democratic revolution, were mostly small and medium craftsmen, traders and merchants, brewers and millers. The most powerful financiers, whose capital contributed in decisive manner to economic activity in Bohemia, lived in Vienna, while the less wealthy financial and industrial middle classes were mostly German. One of the few

The Čertovka, a branch of the River Vltava, made as mill-race in the 12th century, thus forming Kampa Island

The Citizens' Swimming Pool below Letná on the left bank of the Vltava, built by J. Kranner after 1840

The Arrival of the First Train in Prague, coloured etching from the year 1845

exceptions was Vojtěch Lanna, a Czech entrepreneur, who carried out engineering projects on rivers, roads and railway lines. In 1847 he collaborated with the Prague miller Václav Novotný in founding the mines and ironworks at Kladno.

As Czech society in Prague slowly widened aided by immigrants from the countryside who had retained their national tongue, the Revival Movement assumed a different character, changed its ways and attracted increasing numbers of the town's population. After an Enlightened generation of scientists and critics, whose most outstanding member, Josef Dobrovský (1753—1829), reached international renown, the leadership passed to a younger generation of scientists and poets in the early 19th century.

The leader was Josef Jungmann (1772—1847), who gathered around him in Prague, after 1815, a varied group of writers. They professed Prague culture, literature and the other arts of Romanticism, which, in the form of pre-Romanticism, coloured the final years of the 18th century as a lower current of Neo-Classicism.

The broad current of Romanticism penetrated philosophy and all the arts, particularly those concerned with the purest emotions, music and poetry, and it acted as effective catalyser of the National Revival. By stressing the power and impact of the emotions as against cool, enlightened reason, it turned sceptical scientists into ardent patriots, passionately at the service of their nation. Neo-Classicism seeking its patterns in Antiquity was replaced by a cult of the nation and its folk culture, which provided a true, unspoilt source of pure beauty. Romantic Historicism, which turned from Antiquity to the Middle Ages, effectively supported the interests of the Czech Revivalists by pointing to the period of national greatness.

Romanticism gave the Czech Revival Movement great faith in the happy and great future of their nation and relieved them of their feeling of smallness and inferiority, since the National Movement was based on the ideas of Slavonic culture and subsequent political collaboration. It did not matter that irony of history produced the idea of the mission of the Slavs in the future of mankind through the mouth of a German, the Romantic philosopher Johann Gottfried Herder.

In short, Romanticism seemed to pour new blood into the veins of the young Revivalist generation, who worked intensively on a broad basis and created works at a time that was extremely unfavourable and even inimical to the National Movement.

In the thirties of the 19th century Romanticism reached its climax in Prague. It became incorporated in the literature of the following generation, who, by contrast to their older contemporaries, no longer linked science and art and devoted themselves exclusively to poetry, prose or drama. They were marked by the July Revolution in Paris and the November Uprising in Poland in 1830, which stirred the stagnant waters of the Metternich police state.

At the head of the new generation stood the very agile and talented Josef Kajetán Tyl (1808—1856), a poet and prose writer, actor and dramatist, editor and journalist, critic and organizer of social life, but the greatest personality of the time was Karel Hynek Mácha (1810—1836). This most consistent of Czech revolutionary Romantics and radical believer in the ideas of artistic freedom, managed to express the most subtle

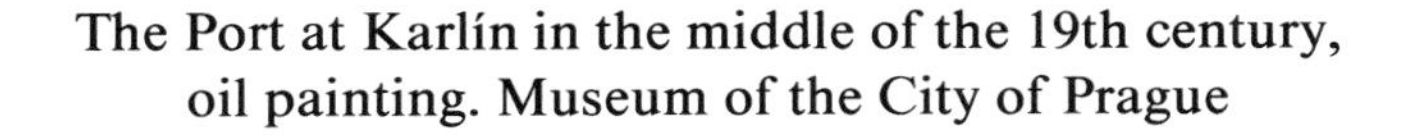
The Port at Karlín in the middle of the 19th century,
oil painting. Museum of the City of Prague

The Empire Kinský Summer Palace in Petřín Park was
built to plans by the architect J. Koch in 1827—1831.
Today the Ethnographical Department
of the National Museum

shades of modern feelings in a delicious, aurally perfectly attuned poetical tongue. He created works with which every new generation of Czech poets has to come to terms.

In the thirties Romanticism became the common base of painting, architecture and the applied arts in Prague. The landscapes of Antonín Mánes (1784—1843) and Josef Navrátil (1798—1865), the religious and historical compositions of František Tkadlík (1786—1840) best represent the original note of Czech Romantic painting, while the greatest Romantic architecture in Prague — the Neo-Gothic building of the Old Town Hall — destroyed in May 1945 — was a dead, inorganic work by Viennese architects, which did not fit sensitively into its historical setting.

The Industrial Revolution, which developed in the forties, the first working class risings in the Smíchov textile mills in 1844 and the arrival of the first locomotive in Prague through tunnels in the city walls in 1845 were harbingers of the new epoch of capitalism, to which the year 1848 opened the doors.

In the forties a number of young writers were active in Prague, who moved from Romanticism to Realism and showed interest in social and political questions. In the first place the journalist, poet and politician Karel Havlíček Borovský (1821—1856) and the woman-writer Božena Němcová (1820—1862). At that time Bedřich Smetana (1824—1884) wrote his early music and painter Josef Mánes (1820—1871) produced his first pictures.

Pre-revolutionary Prague began to change its appearance in the forties of the 19th century. First, it received new lines of communications, made necessary by the growing industries and their need for transportation. Steam ships began to ply the Vltava in 1841. In 1846—1849 the Karlín port was built. In 1839—1941 a chain bridge was hung across the Vltava close to the National Theatre, at the end of what is today Národní street. The project was worked out by Bedřich Schnirch.

On this occasion the old town embankment between the two towns — today's Smetana Embankment — was built up with good taste and artistic forethought, and this created the popular view of the Hradčany panorama with the Lesser Town admired ever since. The first modern regulation of the river was carried out thoroughly. Space was provided for the first Romantic monument in Prague, a Neo-Gothic memorial with allegorical figures of the regions of Bohemia. The equestrian statue of Emperor Franz I, which originally stood there, is today in the depositary of the National Museum. The monument was designed in 1844—1846 by the architect Josef Kranner and carved by the sculptors Josef Max and Josef Böhm.

The oldest Prague station, built by the engineer Jüngling in 1844—1845 for the first steam trains between Prague and Olomouc, stands to this day in Hybernská street and continues to serve as Prague Central Station (nádraží Praha-Střed). In the following years, in 1846—1850, a mighty viaduct was erected on the route Prague-Dresden, the Negrelli Viaduct, which fits well into the landscape.

After 1845 the first town lighting was provided by the gasworks in Karlín. With its 150,000 inhabitants, including suburbs and outlying villages, Prague began slowly to grow into a big industrial town with all the ensuing advantages and shortcomings.

The Lesser Town Cemetery, originally, after 1680, plague cemetery became the public cemetery of the Lesser Town and Hradčany in 1876 and holds a collection of Prague tomb sculpture from the first half of the 19th century. In the centre is the cast-iron tomb of the kneeling Bishop of Passau, Leopold, Count Thun-Hohenstein, a work by V. Prachner, 1831.

A Half Century of Historical Styles

The year 1848 was a historic milestone also in the life of Prague, which became the main scene of all decisive historical encounters from the first March Petition until the suppression of the May Rising in 1849. Yet in a particular historical paradox Prague, which, in comparison with Vienna and Budapest entered the revolution with greatest caution and prudence, was the first to be defeated, even with weapons in hand on the barricades. The June Rising of 1848 was suppressed by the army of General Windischgrätz, and this took away the revolutionary élan of the Prague bourgeois democratic movement before it could fully develop.

Just before the June Rising Prague welcomed the delegates to the first Slavonic Congress, which was to unify all Slavic nations in the Habsburg Monarchy against the all-German endeavours of the Frankfurt Parliament.

It was almost symbolical that the sessions of the Slavonic Congress came to a premature end with the first shots of the Prague Rising. Its defeat caused all the March demands—the independence of the Crown of Bohemia within the monarchy, a Diet of the Crown Lands of Bohemia, central authorities in Prague and the autonomy of the towns and villages — to be buried. The National Council was dissolved, and a state of emergency was declared in Prague.

The fifties of the 19th century passed in the depressing atmosphere of the government of the infamous Minister of the Interior Alexander Bach, and meant a temporary retreat of the Czech National Movement. The police regime, which persecuted any form of liberalism and Czech patriotism, and the advancing Germanization, when German replaced Czech at all offices and schools, did not, however, put a stop to the creativeness of the nation that had been politically roused.

The former Czech Savings Bank, now the Presidium of the Czechoslovak Academy of Sciences, on Národní street, built according to a plan by the architect I. Ullmann in 1858—1861

The House "At the Chestnut Tree" in Břevnov

In the fifties two most beautiful books were published—*Bouquet* (Kytice) by Karel Jaromír Erben, and *Grandmother* (Babička) by Božena Němcová. At that time Karel Havlíček Borovský was writing his satirical works but these were not printed until after the author's death, when his funeral in Prague in 1856 became a national demonstration against the police regime in Vienna.

A year before Bach's absolutism the young generation of writers associated around the *May* Almanach began to publish their works. They followed up the heritage of the Romantic poet K. H. Mácha and of Erben, Němcová and Havlíček. This generation was led by the realistic and democratic writer Jan Neruda (1834—1891), and for several decades these writers stood at the van of cultural life in Prague, trying to raise it to the level of European culture.

A number of painters shared the ideas of the literary generation and their endeavours to catch up on Europe. They were Realists, who had established contact with West European art during study trips to Belgium and France, where they adopted Realism as their own form of expression in art (Karel Purkyně, Soběslav Pinkas, Jaroslav Čermák). In the fifties the work of the painter Josef Mánes reached its climax, and a whole generation of Czech landscape painters were busy at work, the most talented among whom, Adolf Kosárek, died prematurely in 1859.

Bach's absolutism was not a mere continuation of the Metternich absolutism before the revolution in 1848. He suppressed almost every achievement of the revolution, but by upholding the abolition of serfdom and equality before the law, he opened the way to the further development of capitalism and the full impact of the Industrial Revolution. Within a short time this turned Bohemia into the most highly industrialized country of the Habsburg Empire.

The textile industry of the middle of the 19th century was now replaced by heavy industry,

The Petřín View-Tower of 1891, a copy of the Eiffel Tower in Paris, 60 metres high

The Church of SS Cyril and Methodius in Karlín, designed by the Viennese architect K. Rössner in collaboration with the Prague architect V. I. Ullmann, 1854—1863

the growth of which supported the introduction of machinery into production and the speedy spread of railway transport. In 1852 the Ringhofer Plant for the Production of Railway Carriages was opened at Smíchov. In 1854 Č. Daněk founded a factory producing sugar refinery equipment, which after merger with the Breitfeld and Evans Works in 1872 and the Czech-Moravian Kolben Engineering Works in 1928, grew into today's nationalized ČKD Concern. Large-scale factory production presented a threat to crafts work; the new Trading Order of 1859 put an end to the guilds and legalized free enterprise.

Thus the fifties opened up a new epoch of capitalist economy in Prague: large factories grew up, the railway network became denser, a nation-wide market was established, and the first limited companies came into existence. The economic crisis of 1857 did not put a brake on expending economic life for long, which, in the sixties, reached a period of unheard-of boom.

In the fifties the number of inhabitants in Prague rose steeply, and it doubled within thirty years. Inner Prague became an overcrowded city, and the suburban areas caught up rapidly. The growing need for accommodation led to extensive building activity, which was in the hands of contractors, and speculators did not respect any town planning or aesthetic concerns. Class differentiation showed clearly in this building boom when ugly tenement houses with galleries, small flats and insufficient hygienic facilities went up in the Žižkov district while, in Vinohrady, apartment houses were constructed with large comfortable flats for wealthier inhabitants. Artistically demanding architecture found a place only on isolated occasions, mainly on private houses.

By contrast to Karlín, Smíchov and Holešovice, Žižkov and Vinohrady were built largely as residential quarters without large industrial plants. Originally, in 1849, the whole territory east of the walls of the New Town was named Vinohrady, referring to the one-time vineyards that spread here from the 14th to 18th century. In 1875 the more southerly parts of Vinohrady were divided off from the northern part below Vítkov Hill and after 1877 this separate district began to be called Žižkov and was raised to the status of town in 1881. Vinohrady, which grew up around Vinohradská street, a prolongation of Wenceslas Square, became a town in 1879; all the lovely parks were completely destroyed during its growth, which came to a climax in the nineties of the 19th and in the early 20th century. A number of civic buildings were built, and apartment houses appeared around the main square, today's Peace Square (náměstí Míru).

The building boom continued in the sixties of the 19th century after the fall of Bach's police regime and the passing of the so-called October Diploma of 1860, in which Emperor Franz Joseph I renounced absolutism for once and all, promised to acknowledge the political rights of the Czech nation and to keep to a future Constitution.

The first half of the sixties witnessed an unheard-of development in Prague life, full of political, social and cultural events which involved the establishment of choirs, art and physical training unions and the instigation of new political trends and parties, bitter election campaigns and nationality struggles. The relaxation of political conditions had a favourable influence also on Czech literature and art.

But the joyful enthusiasm, stimulated by the rebirth of hopes, was soon cooled by the Austro-Prussian War and the occupation of Prague by the Prussians in 1866 and its consequences, the Austro-Hungarian Settlement of 1867, which granted autonomy to Hungary but completely ignored the statutory rights of Bohemia. When the Emperor rejected the Fundamental Articles, in which the Czechs, in 1871, demanded their political and nationality rights, patriotic enthusiasm began to recede, and Czech political life underwent an internal crisis. At the same time, the economy suffered a crisis. In 1873 the state went bankrupt, and the subsequent stagnation was not overcome by industry until the eighties.

The National Theatre, the most important work of architecture of the 19th century, built to plans by the architect Josef Zítek in 1869—1881 and finished after a fire in 1881 by the architect Josef Schulz. Leading Czech artists contributed to the sculptural and painted decorations.

When in 1866 Prague was proclaimed an open city and the Prussians occupied it, it ceased to be a fortress, and its fortifications lost their significance. Emperor Franz Joseph I had promised the citizens of Prague that he would donate the walls to them, but he did not keep his word—nor the later promise of his coronation as King of Bohemia. And since the government in Vienna assumed a negative attitude to the demands that the Prague fortifications should be pulled down — as they did in regard to the completion of the railway network and the links between the town and its suburbs — in the end the Prague community had to purchase the walls at great cost in 1871 and began pulling them down by stages after 1874.

In this way it became possible to link up Karlín, Žižkov, Vinohrady, Smíchov and the other more outlying parts with inner Prague, to which only Vyšehrad (1883), Holešovice (1884) and Libeň (1901) were added later. The other larger suburban communities were, on the contrary, raised to the status of independent towns which, understandably, complicated the possibility of finding a satisfactory solution to their common problem how to build up Prague as a modern metropolis. The demolition of the walls in the seventies stimulated the modernization of the transport system. In 1875 the Prague horse tram began operating, and in 1891 it was replaced by electric trams.

The 1848 Revolution put a stop to the nobility's building enterprise in architecture. There now appeared the style of the Second Baroque or Rococo as an expression of the wealthy middle classes. With this style the burghers set out to copy the feudal aristocracy just as they wanted to acquire coats-of-arms and aristocratic titles. The Baroque shapes and ornaments on the burghers' houses were, therefore, exaggerated out of all proportion and stressed to such a degree that the builder's social status and his newly acquired wealth should be clear to all.

The builder J. Malický was a representative of this style. He designed a number of apartment houses and, in the fifties and sixties, also the building of the Law Court on the Fruit Market (1850—1852) and Stallburg Palace (1861—1862) in Panská street in the New Town.

A style that suited the views and feelings of the middle class builders far better was the Neo-Renaissance, derived from the West European and particularly Italian Renaissance. Since the middle classes now entirely replaced the nobility in their urge to erect buildings, this style was far closer to them than the feudal Baroque.

The demands of the Prague bourgeoisie for representative civic buildings and intimate private houses of various type and purpose were ideally satisfied by the architect V. Ignaz Ullmann (1822—1897). Apart from participating in the project for the Neo-Romanesque Church of SS Cyril and Methodius in Karlín, he designed the Neo-Renaissance Lanna Palace in Hybernská street (1857), the building of the Bohemian Savings Banks (1858—1861) — today the Presidium of the Czechoslovak Academy of Sciences, and the adjacent Lažan Palace (1861—1863) — today the Slavia Coffee

The curtain of the National Theatre in Prague by Vojtěch Hynais, 1883. It allegorically depicts the building of the theatre with the collaboration of the entire Czech nation.

House and Film Faculty of the Academy of Musical Arts (on Národní street opposite the National Theatre), the building of the Provisional Theatre (1862) at the back of the National Theatre, the Girls' High School in Vodičkova street (1867), still a school today, and the building of the Czech University of Technology on Charles Square — today Faculty of Machine Engineering. He designed a number of other buildings in the same style, ranging from the Sokol Gymnasium in Sokolská street in the New Town (1863—1864), and a restaurant on Letná Plain (1863) to Lanna Villa in Dejvice (1870).

V. I. Ullmann was trained at the Vienna Academy. In the majority of his designs he used the pattern of the Italian Renaissance but managed to make use of French stimuli and the local Renaissance tradition to create works that fulfilled the period need for representative and intimate architecture, which always perfectly served its purpose.

His brother-in-law and at first collaborator, Antonín Barvitius (1823—1910), was also trained in Vienna. He spent thirteen years in Italy and enriched Prague with two exceptional buildings of remarkable artistic level. His design for the villa of factory-owner Moritz Gröbe (1879—1881) at the border of Vinohrady and Vršovice, surrounded by a terraced garden with fountains and grottos, was one of those happily conceived works that roused a lively memory of sunny Italy in each visitor. His later work was St Wenceslas' Basilica in Smíchov (1881—1885). It has a Neo-Renaissance exterior, and is one of the most beautiful Prague churches of the last century, harmonious in proportions.

While architect Josef Hlávka (1831—1908), later one of Prague's great patrons of the arts, designed and built the Prague Maternity Home in the style of English Late Gothic (1867—1875), his contemporary Josef Zítek (1832—1909) gave to Prague the culminating work of the Czech Neo-Renaissance, and artistically the most progressive work of architecture of the entire 19th century: the building of the National Theatre (1865—1881).

Its construction meant for Prague and the entire Czech nation far more than the mere establishment of a theatre. The Czech people regarded this theatre as a true temple of national re-birth, a monument to the culmination of the revival of Czech culture, the most striking proof of the renewal and full and rich life of the nation. The common people willingly made small contribution towards the building construction when the Viennese government refused support, because each of them desired to share in this great patriotic achievement.

Even though Josef Zítek did not deny his Viennese training in his design — his professors were the architects of the Viennese Court Opera — he managed to overcome all the difficulties and disadvantages of the given site and create a monumental work of architecture composed with great sensibility. He worked out each external façade in a different manner according to its function in the setting to achieve a perfect view from far off, from across the river, and from closeby. He crowned the entire building with a soaring curving cupola, which reminds Prague not so much of Italian Palladian architecture as of the Royal Summer Palace, the Belvedere at Prague Castle. Compared with the Court Opera in Vienna the National Theatre is a far more popular building.

Josef Zítek, as a true Neo-Renaissance architect, from the beginning counted on the cooperation of a large number of sculptors and painters in decorating this important building and gathered around him a whole generation of Prague artists, most of them graduates of the Prague Academy.

The cycle *My Country* by Mikoláš Aleš, the mural and ceiling allegories by František Ženíšek in the foyer (the two painters jointly entered the competition for the decorations of the National Theatre), Ženíšek's *Allegory of Art* on the ceiling of the auditorium, and the frescoes by Josef Tulka in the lunettes of the loggia follow Mánes' tradition. On the other hand, different art trends of the eighties and nineties were expressed on the curtain by Vojtěch Hynais, his pictures on the staircase to the Royal box and its salon, Václav Brožík's historical compositions and the famous landscapes of Bohemia by Julius Mařák in the salon and ante-chamber to the royal box. Sculptural decorations were supplied by Bohuslav Schnirch, Antonín Wagner and Josef Václav Myslbek.

The National Theatre thus became a treasure house of Czech art in the last decade of the 19th century. It is to be regretted that J. Zítek with his Neo-Renaissance restraint did not permit the most original personalities, sculptor J. V. Myslbek and painter M. Aleš, to take a more conspicuous part in the theatre decorations.

After the unfortunate fire of the National Theatre in 1881 J. Zítek parted ways with the building commission, and the final adaptations to the building were carried out by his colleague Josef Schulz (1840—1917). Together these two architects designed the dignified House of Artists on the embankment with its splendid concert hall. The building was named Rudolphinum in honour of the successor to the throne, Archduke Rudolph, the only son of Emperor Franz Joseph I.

Schulz's architectural work culminated in the immense building of the National Museum, with its exaggerated proportions following the pattern of the Vienna museums, and inspired by the Paris Louvre. It encloses the upper end of Wenceslas Square. The National Museum, too, was of greater importance in its representative rather than functional purpose and gave opportunities to sculptors and painters who shared in its decoration. One part of the building is a Pantheon (1885—1890) with statues of

The House of Artists, originally called the Rudolphinum, on Red Army Square, the work of architects J. Zítek and J. Schulz in 1876—1884. Today the home of the Czech Philharmonic Orchestra and the Academy of Music

The National Museum, built to a design
by Josef Schulz in 1885—1890

famous Czech personalities but the artistic level does not reach up to the standard of the sculpture and painting in the National Theatre. The cupola of the Pantheon, however, forms one of the dominating features of the city.

Schulz's third Prague building, the Museum of Decorative Arts (Uměleckoprůmyslové muzeum) opposite the Rudolphinum (1897—1900), is less pompous and more agreeable in its architecture. It was designed in the style of the French Neo-Renaissance. The building is surrounded by the old Jewish Cemetery, bordered, on one side, by the Late Gothic Pinkas Synagogue and, on the other, by the Early Baroque Klaus Synagogue. Both these synagogues are today part of the State Jewish Museum and some of the valuable collections are exhibited there.

In the seventies of the 19th century Prague became linked to its suburbs de facto if not legally, and this laid the foundations for the future Greater Prague. It was an important period of transition in economic, political and cultural life.

A striking change occurred in literature and the arts. In 1877 the poet Josef Václav Sládek became editor of the *Lumír* journal and with his colleagues Julius Zeyer and Jaroslav Vrchlický began to place stress not on unilateral national standpoints but on a broader orientation in world literature and purely artistic values. The generation of classical Czech painters and sculptors created their last culminating works in the sixties. They were followed in the seventies by the Generation of the National Theatre, and, at that time, saw the birth of the first generation of modern Czech art, Art Nouveau and Symbolism.

The most outstanding achievement of the seventies was that of composer Bedřich Smetana, who set an example of national and simultaneously world art. In his music he managed to express the basic qualities of the Czech nation and their most noble longings. In the operas *Dalibor* (1867) and *Libuše* (1872), his symphonic poems *Vyšehrad* and *Vltava* (1874—1879) and the whole cycle *My Country* Smetana glorified Prague, the town he lived in, where he worked and was active in public life. He did this in such an impressive and convincing a manner that his music, to this day, most perfectly expresses the spiritual life of Prague and must be regarded as the most outstanding achievement ever created in the city.

In the eighties the social and artistic contradictions grew more acute. The crisis of Czech political life was clear for all to see. In 1882 Czech lectures began to be given at the still divided Charles-Ferdinand University, and soon a new generation of Czech scientists initiated the struggle against all forms of petty bourgeois and false patriotism throughout the nation.

Within the framework of the Neo-Renaissance style a trend known as Czech Renaissance developed in the eighties, which found its stimulus in local Renaissance architecture of the second half of the 16th century and produced smooth sgraffito façades and picturesque gables. The creator of this national trend, which reflects the growing

The Pantheon of the National Museum, devoted to great personalities of the Czech nation, who are represented in bronze busts by leading Czech sculptors

The grand stairways of the National Museum, designed by the architect Josef Schulz in 1885—1890

Karel Purkyně, The Family of Count Thurn-Taxis on the Ice, oil painting, 1858. National Gallery, Prague

cultural needs of the economically developing Czech burghers' society, was Zítek's disciple, architect Antonín Wiehl (1846—1910), who collaborated with the painter Mikoláš Aleš as a designer of the cartons for the sgraffito decorations.

In 1883 Antonín Wiehl built the Old Town waterworks near Charles Bridge in the style of this Czech Renaissance. Today it serves as the Smetana Museum. The sgraffito was made according to cartons by F. Ženíšek and M. Aleš. In 1889 Wiehl erected the apartment house at the corner of Jilská and Skořepka streets in the Old Town with sgraffito by M. Aleš. In 1896 he built his own house on Wenceslas Square where today the Academia Publishing House is to be found. This, too, has paintings designed by M. Aleš on the façade.

Wiehl derived his inspiration from the Italian Late Renaissance when, in 1887, he designed the arcades of the Vyšehrad Cemetery, the burial place of the most outstanding personalities of the Czech nation. In 1890 he drew up the blueprints for the former City Savings Bank in Rytířská street in the Old Town. This building — now the Gottwald Museum — came into being in collaboration with the architect Osvald Polívka. It was the first civic building in Prague which was deliberately constructed exclusively by Czech artists and out of Czech materials. A. Wiehl founded a school of architecture in Prague, whose members soon abandoned Neo-Renaissance for Neo-Baroque, and some went on to Art Nouveau.

Viktor Barvitius, Thursday in Stromovka Park, oil painting, 1864. National Gallery, Prague

Josef Navrátil, The Italian on the Shop Sign of the Delicatessen Shop "Zum Italiener" in Železná street, No. 548, in the Old Town, oil on metal. National Gallery, Prague

Ctirad and Šárka, statue by Josef Václav Myslbek, 1889—1897, originally sited on Palacký Bridge, today in the park at Vyšehrad

Slavín, the burial place of outstanding personalities in Czech culture at the Vyšehrad cemetery, built after a design by the architect A. Wiehl in 1889—1890, sculptural collaboration by J. Mauder

Transformation in the Modern Age

František Palacký, Portrait Bust of an Art Nouveau Memorial, made by the sculptor Stanislav Sucharda in collaboration with the architect Alois Dryák in 1905—1907

The Foundation of the Metropolis

Prague entered the 20th century as a large industrial town, which spared no efforts to grow into a modern European metropolis despite all hurdles placed in its way by the government in Vienna and the consequences of its preceding building history.

The main obstacle was the administrative division of the Prague territory, which prevented the implementation of large-scale town planning requirements as needed by the modern era. The town kept growing as the result of the constant inflow of the rural population, which changed the ratio of Czech at the expense of the German inhabitants. The large suburban settlements, from 1879 on, gradually became independent townships and outdid in the number of inhabitants the inner city, which was overcrowded already in the eighties.

In the second half of the 19th century the urgent need to link up the settlements on both sides of the Vltava led to the construction of new bridges. Franz Joseph I Chain Bridge (1865—1868) at the end of present-day Revoluční street, the Holešovice Bridge, demolished in 1947 and replaced by the modern Šverma Bridge (Švermův most), and the Iron Foot-Bridge (1868—1870) not far from today's Mánes Bridge (Mánesův most) were followed in 1876—1878 by Palacký Bridge (Palackého most). This was decorated at the corners with four statues by J. V. Myslbek (1889—1897)

Art Nouveau Monument to Master Jan Hus on the Old Town Square, the work of the sculptor Ladislav Šaloun, 1903—1915

Mosaic called Homage to Prague, in a niche above the main entrance to the Municipal House on the Republic Square, made according to a carton by Karel Špillar in 1911

representing Libuše and Přemysl, Lumír and Song on the New Town side and Ctirad and Šárka, Záboj and Slavoj on the Smíchov side. This statuary is now to be found in the park at Vyšehrad.

Other bridges followed in the 20th century, before the outbreak of the First World War. Franz Joseph I Bridge (1899—1901) near the National Theatre was designed by the architect Antonín Balšánek and is today called the May-Day Bridge (most Prvního máje). Enginner Jiří Soukup and the architect Jan Koula built Svatopluk Čech Bridge (most Svatopluka Čecha, 1905—1908) at the end of Pařížská street. Hlávka Bridge (Hlávkův most), which crosses Štvanice Island, was built in 1908—1912 according to a design by the architect Pavel Janák with the sculptures of Humanity and Labour on the Holešovice pylons (Jan Štursa) and medallions by Josef Mařatka and Otto Gutfreund. Franz Ferdinand Bridge (1911—1914) near the Rudolphinum was the work of engineers František Mencl and Alois Nový in collaboration with the architect Mečislav Petrů. Today it is called Mánes Bridge.

The development of the Prague industrial districts involved not only the layout of new streets and construction of tenement houses but also the provision of gasworks, electric power stations, water mains and sewerage, the building of schools and other civic

The Art Nouveau Main Station built to plans by the architect Josef Fanta 1901—1909

facilities. In 1895 the town waterworks were built in Podolí (enlarged in 1896 and reconstructed to its present form in 1929—1931 according to a design by the architect Antonín Engel). Holešovice became one of the liveliest districts in Prague with the building of the central slaughterhouse (1893—1895), the power-station (1897—1902), new industrial plants, a fairground (1891) and a port (1893—1894). Libeň also saw the construction of a new port (1894) and an electric tramway, which linked the rapidly growing industrial district with the inner city.

The residential districts of Vinohrady and Žižkov grew up without any town plan which might take into account the undulating ground. The present appearance is the result of chance private enterprise and mechanical designs by engineers without the participation of any artists. Finally it was the need to complete the construction of these two separate towns with church building that gave the architects their opportunity to intervene artistically. The two Neo-Gothic Churches of St Procopius (sv. Prokop) in Žižkov (1899—1903) and St Ludmila in Vinohrady (1883—1903), designed by the architect Josef Mocker, are, however, examples of non-creative, cold and schematic Pseudo-Gothic works designed on the drawing board.

In comparison with the rapid development of the town and the villages on the outskirts, the unbearable condition of the inner city became increasingly obvious. Its medieval ground plan and built-up area suited the ancient way of life and prevented modernization. For that reason major clearance work was undertaken in Prague in 1893. Its purpose was to remove the unhygienic and unfit housing conditions and to make room for new building enterprise. In the Old Town this clearance affected, in the first place, the Old Jewish Joseph Quarter (Josefov), in the New Town the Adalbert Quarter around the Church of St Adalbert (sv. Vojtěch) below the National Theatre, and the old Podskalí ("Below the Rock" district) north of Vyšehrad.

The most aggravating conditions had prevailed in the former Jewish ghetto, whose narrow and winding streets with numerous receding buildings and corners, blind alleys, passageways and later additions were the result of organic growth of an early medieval town and the intricate ownership rights inside the ghetto. When the clearance was over during the First World War there remained of the original complex of 288 houses only the Old-New Synagogue (Staronová synagoga), the oldest in Europe, the Rococo Jewish Town Hall — originally Gothic and rebuilt in the Renaissance period — the town hall synagogue called the High Synagogue (Vysoká synagoga) and the old Jewish Cemetery with the Pinkas and the Klaus Synagogues.

All these monuments, however, were drowned by new apartment houses. These new houses provided modern, comfortable living quarters but had façades, where motifs of all possible historical styles were applied without good taste.

The clearance was basically correct and had become essential to the living organism of the town. But it stimulated feverish building enterprise, where no regard was paid to the historical development of Prague and the monuments of the past nor to the aesthetic demands of contemporary modern art.

It must, consequently, be regarded as lucky that lack of funds prevented further insensitive building enterprise in Prague. Even so the clearance did irreparable damage to the historical body of Prague, and this barbarian destruction was rightly and hotly condemned by the Czech intellectuals.

Art Nouveau houses of the former Prague Insurance Company and Publisher Topič (today Publishing House of the Czechoslovak Union of Writers) on Národní street, designed by Osvald Polívka, c. 1910

Neo-Baroque, Art Nouveau, Cubism

The nineties of the 19th century and the early 20th century brought Prague closer to the advanced European cities, both economically and culturally. The Jubilee Industrial Exhibition in Stromovka Park in 1891 — held on the occasion of the hundredth anniversary of the first industrial exhibition in Prague — showed that Bohemia was keeping step with the leading industrial countries. In 1896 engineer Emil Kolben founded a factory for electro-technical machinery in Vysočany, which supplied equipment to many European and overseas power-stations. In 1900 the production of locomotives was started in the Czech-Moravian Engineering Works. And in 1907 the Praga Automobile Works came into existence.

Prague industry kept up its prosperity even during the difficult years of the nineties, when there were export problems and after the economic crisis in the early 20th century. Prague was well ahead of the other towns of Austria-Hungary in a new field, cinematography, when J. Kříženecký, in 1898, presented his first documentary news reels.

The growth of industry, trade and transport meant that the number of Prague workers more than doubled in the last quarter of the 19th century. This obviously strengthened the position of the Social Democratic Party, which concentrated on the struggle to win a general franchise.

In 1893 a people's demonstration took place in Prague in support of the general franchise. The police and army intervened, and a state of emergency was proclaimed. A new wave of mass demonstrations in support of the general franchise arose in 1905. Finally the government gave in, and in the 1907 elections the first six social democratic

Art Nouveau Villa of the sculptor František Bílek in Mickiewiczova street in Hradčany, built of bricks according to the artist's own design in 1911 and symbolizing a corn field

Moses, bronze sculpture by František Bílek, 1905,
in the park in front of the Old-New Synagogue
in the former Jewish Town of Prague

deputies were elected into the general representative body. But tension did not decrease, on the contrary, it intensified until the outbreak of the war.

The last decades before the First World War found Prague a metropolis with a high level of culture and with great and deliberate striving to create modern arts. In 1895 — two years before the Vienna Jugendstil emerged — a *Manifesto of Prague Modern Artists* was published, in which young Czech poets headed by critic F. X. Šalda proclaimed freedom of art and criticism, the development of creative individuality as opposed to narrow-minded patriotism. That same year the *Modern Revue* began to appear in Prague, a literary journal of Decadent poets with Symbolist leanings, and a year later the *Art Nouveau Almanach* associating modern poets of various trends and creeds.

In political life the traditional political parties of the "Old" and "New Bohemians" were now opposed by new parties (the National Socialist, the Christian Socialist, the Agrarian and the People's Party). Similarly, in literature and art there emerged many

Detail of a stained glass window in the Choir of St Vitus' Cathedral, designed by Max Švabinský, 1946—1947

currents, groups and individual forms, which, in original manner and expression, kept pace with contemporary art in Western Europe. Paris became the promised city and, in the second half of the 19th century, artists went to study and gain inspiration there increasingly often and in growing numbers.

And since national Czech art was based on local tradition it received a mighty impulse from a grand Ethnographical Exhibition held in 1895. Soon a new and attractive centre of culture and art arose once again in Prague, and individual and contradictory trends and views met here, mutually stimulated each other and gained in strength. After Bedřich Smetana, the sculptor Josef Václav Myslbek and painter Mikoláš Aleš, the most important personality in Prague at the end of the 19th century was the composer Antonín Dvořák (1841—1904), who took Czech music out into the world and whose works enchant the world to this day. Another outstanding composer was Zdeněk Fibich (1850—1900). The younger generation of musicians, who worked in the early 20th century and followed up the heritage of Smetana and Dvořák, did not produce their culminating works until after the First World War.

In the nineties art in Prague was borne by a generation of artists who can be called the Art Nouveau Generation according to the prevailing trends of the time, even though their members were concerned also with Naturalism, Impressionism, and Symbolism. The young generation was organized in the Mánes Union of Artists, and the *Free Trends* journal (Volné směry) was their spokesman. Leading artists included the figure painter Jan Preisler (1872—1918), landscape painter Antonín Slavíček (1870—1910), the sculptors Stanislav Sucharda (1866—1916) and František Bílek (1872—1941). The Art Nouveau generation includes, among others, the founder of Art Nouveau, Alfons Mucha (1860—1939), and one of the classical painters of abstract art, František Kupka (1871—1957).

In architecture the nineties saw the encounter of Historical Styles (Eclecticism) with the Neo-Renaissance alternating with Neo-Baroque, and New Styles, deliberately anti-historical in character, in particular Art Nouveau.

Wenceslas Square, the main thoroughfare in Prague, originally the Horse Market, set up by Charles IV in 1348, the venue of important historical events. At its top end stands the St Wenceslas Monument, with the Patron Saints of Bohemia, Ludmila, Procopius, Agnes and Adalbert, the most important work by J. V. Myslbek, 1912—1924

Cubist House "At the Black Mother of God" at the corner of Celetná street and the Fruit Market in the Old Town, the work of the architect Josef Gočár, 1911—1912

Cubist villas at the foot of Vyšehrad, built according to a design by the architect Josef Chochol 1913

Cubist apartment house in Neklanova street,
No. 98, at Vyšehrad, designed by the
architect J. Chochol in 1913

While in 1894 the architect Osvald Polívka designed the building of the Land Bank in the style of the Czech Renaissance, at the very same time (1893—1894) an enormous Neo-Baroque building of the former Straka Academy was built on the Lesser Town bank according to a design by the architect Václav Roštlapil. Today it is used by the Presidium of the Government of the Czechoslovak Socialist Republic.

The first Art Nouveau buildings in Prague were designed by the Viennese architect Bedřich Ohmann (Corso Coffee House, 1897—1898, which used to stand on Na Příkopě street, the Central Hotel in Hybernská street, 1900, now the Chamber Theatre — Komorní divadlo). Ohmann, too, was an adherent of Neo-Baroque and designed a number of other Prague buildings in that style, including Walter Palace in Voršilská street (1894—1895) — today the Papal Nunciatur, the interior of the Variety Theatre (1893—1898) — now the Music Theatre in Karlín, and Kramář Villa on the Castle Bastion (1909).

All leading Prague architects slowly turned to Art Nouveau. It was the first original artistic style of the rich burghers that did not copy the old art forms of the aristocratic styles but formed patterns of its own derived from nature. This generation was led by Jan Kotěra (1871—1923), who designed an apartment house on Wenceslas Square

(1899) for factory-owner Peterka and the wooden Exhibition Pavilion of the Mánes Union below Kinský Gardens (1902) — now demolished — used for the Rodin Exhibition in 1902.

In the first years of the 20th century a number of remarkable Art Nouveau buildings went up in Prague, civic buildings, apartment houses and private villas, both in the inner city and the suburbs. The most important were designed by Josef Fanta (Franz Joseph Station, 1901—1911, today Prague Main Station) and by Osvald Polívka and Antonín Balšánek (The Municipal House — Obecní dům — on the Republic Square, 1906—1911). J. Fanta designed the building of the Prague Hlahol Union on Gottwald Embankment (1905), O. Polívka the U Nováků building in Vodičkova street (1902—1903), the house of the former Prague Insurance Company and the adjacent building — today the Publishing House of the Czechoslovak Union of Writers on Národní street (1910). In the middle of Wenceslas Square stands the Art Nouveau Evropa Hotel built according to the plans by Ohmann's disciple, architect Bedřich Bendlmayer (1903—1905). Whole blocks of apartment houses in the centre of Prague and elsewhere and entire villa districts were built in Art Nouveau Style.

The most original of these Art Nouveau works is the villa of the sculptor František Bílek (1911), who designed it himself and used the symbolism of a "cornfield" in the ground plan and on the columns — loose, supporting and broken ears of corn — and similarly on the details of doors, wrought metal work, stone lintels and interior furnishings.

Art Nouveau broadened the streets in the newly built villa quarters, enlarged the spaces between houses and filled the resultant area with the green of gardens and avenues of

Bohumil Kubišta, The Quarry at Braník, oil painting, 1910—1911. National Gallery, Prague

Bohumil Kubišta, Old Prague Motif, oil painting, 1911.
National Gallery, Prague

trees. The inner ground-plan of houses, so stiff in the period of the historical styles, loosened and light and air penetrated into the modern homes, the flats became comfortable and functional dwelling places.

The period of Art Nouveau enriched Prague with two monuments of vast size, the Palacký monument by Stanislav Sucharda (1905—1912) in the New Town close to Palacký Bridge and the monument to Master Jan Hus by Ladislav Šaloun (1903—1915) on the Old Town Square, which, to this day, leave a mighty artistic impression with their symbolism and sculptural form.

The most representative building of Prague Art Nouveau is the Municipal House, which was decorated and furnished exclusively by Czech artists, painters A. Mucha, J. Preis-

The Law Faculty of Charles University by Svatopluk Čech Bridge, built by the architect L. Machoň 1928—1929 to a design by the architect J. Kotěra of 1919

Institute of Scientific and Technical Information for Agriculture in Slezská street in Vinohrady, the work of Josef Gočár, 1924—1926

Adria Palace, originally the building of the Riunione Adriatica Insurance Company, built by the architect Pavel Janák, 1923—1924, in collaboration with Josef Zasch. Since 1960 the popular Magic Lantern Theatre holds its performances here.

ler, M. Švabinský, K. Špillar, F. Ženíšek, sculptors L. Šaloun, K. Novák, and various craftsmen. It was not yet finished when the founder of modern Czech architecture, Jan Kotěra, designed his own Prague villa in Vinohrady (1908) entirely void of Art Nouveau decorations and placed the main stress on the purpose and construction, closed shape and the use of pure building materials, mainly unplastered bricks. He applied the same anti-Art Nouveau principles on Laichter House in Vinohrady (1909), the house of the publisher Urbánek — the Mozarteum — in Jungmannova street (1911—1913), the building of the General Pensions Institute on the Engels Embankment (1912—1913) — today the Ministry of Communications, and on his project for the Law Faculty of Charles University and Čech Bridge (Čechův most, after 1914).

Besides these modern buildings Prague acquired several outstanding Cubist works of architecture in the years just before the outbreak of the First World War. They are the more remarkable for having no like anywhere in the world. The introduction of Cubism into architecture was due to a group of young Czech architects, who, together with the Cubist painters Emil Filla, Vincenc Beneš, Antonín Procházka, Josef Čapek, Václav Špála, and the Cubist sculptor Otto Gutfreund, set up a Group of Artists in 1911, whose common aim was Cubism.

The architects Pavel Janák, Vlastislav Hofman and Josef Chochol not only justified Cubism theoretically, but in collaboration with Josef Gočár applied it in practice, even though not every one of them was given the same opportunity. In this regard

Monument to the poet Svatopluk Čech in Čech Gardens at Vinohrady, the work of the sculptor Jan Štursa, in collaboration with the architect Pavel Janák, 1924

Josef Chochol was the most successful (1880—1956). Five Cubist apartment houses were built to his design in Neklanova street below Vyšehrad after 1913, a corner villa by the Railway Bridge and three houses near the Vyšehrad tunnel. Their façades are sculpturally subdivided, each one in a different manner, and effectively use the Cubist motif of the dynamic pyramid.

Josef Gočár (1880—1945) showed convincingly on his House "At the Black Mother of God" (U černé Matky boží, 1911—1912), at the corner of the Fruit Market and Celetná street in the Old Town, that Cubist architecture can fit perfectly into an old Baroque setting without abandoning any of the modern principles of art. This won him patrons in Prague so that he was able to build a semi-detached Cubist house with a striking portal in Tycho de Brahe street in Hradčany.

Although Pavel Janák (Hlávka Bridge—Hlávkův most) and Vlastislav Hofman (the column with the lantern on Jungmann Square—Jungmannovo náměstí) did less work they joined the other Cubist architects in concentrating on designing Cubist household furnishing and set up a special Prague Art Workshops for this purpose. They understood Cubism as a style whose character and typical features were to pervade all forms of art and give shape to the modern environment. Their creative endeavours were interrupted by the outbreak of the First World War, which changed the face of all Europe and radically altered the destiny of Prague.

Greater Prague — the Capital City of the Czechoslovak Republic

Prague suffered greatly during the First World War. It made heavy sacrifices in human lives, suffered hunger and population growth slowed down; building activity came to a stop, and industry turned to producing war supplies. But neither persecution nor lack of food could silence the oppositon to both the war and the government in Vienna. The faster the Austrian war economy declined and the living conditions of the people of Prague grew worse, the more often did demonstrations and strikes break out, acquiring increasing anti-regime characteristics.

The disintegration of Austria-Hungary, its military defeat, the resistance of the Czech nation to the Habsburg Monarchy, foreign campaigns by Professor T. G. Masaryk, and the fight of Czech and Slovak legionaries against the Central Powers, all combined to prepare favourable conditions, under the influence of the Russian Revolution in 1917, for the independence of the Czech state and Slovakia. And once again Prague became an important venue of far-reaching political events. On 28 October 1918 Austria-Hungary capitulated, the independence of Czechoslovakia was proclaimed on Wenceslas Square, and Prague was raised to become the capital city of the newly emerging country, the Czechoslovak Republic.

Charles IV and Peter Parler laying the Foundation Stone to Prague Cathedral, relief on the central door of St Vitus' Cathedral, modelled by Otakar Španiel in 1927—1929 to a carton by V. H. Brunner

The lighthouse tower at Barrandov with a coffee-house and restaurant, built to a design by architect Max Urban in 1927

Dr Müller's Constructivist Villa at Střešovice, designed by the architects Adolf Loos and Karel Lhota, 1929—1920

After three centuries Prague again became residential city even though it was the President of the Republic that resided at Prague Castle and no longer a King of Bohemia. There never was any doubt as to its role since there was no town on the entire territory to compete both in historical tradition and in size, political, economic and cultural importance.

As in the past, so after 1918 the flowering of Prague was stimulated mainly by its function as capital city of the country and headquarters of the highest representatives of the nation. Here were to be found the government and ministries, the sessions of parliament took place here, the ambassadors and consuls of foreign countries worked here, all central authorities were located in the town, the headquarters of the political parties, and their publishing houses, the leading economic, scientific, technical, social and cultural institutions, banks, universities, art unions and sports facilities. And every one of these authorities, enterprises and institutions needed buildings that might suit their purpose and represent them adequately.

Promising perspectives opened up before architects, but there arose one great dilemma. The new country had to chose the way it was to follow. The strongest political party after the war was the Social Democratic Party, but when its right-wing leaders joined up with the bourgeoisie, they managed to suppress the left-wing by force in 1920 and so the political orientation of Czechoslovakia was decided upon until the Second World War. The majority of Czech and Slovak intellectuals held left-wing views, and the progressive Prague architects found themselves faced with a dilemma that was difficult to solve. Inspired by the ideas of Socialism, they had to implement their projects under capitalist conditions.

The Constructivist building of the Prague City Transport Services at Holešovice, built to a project by the architects Adolf Benš and Josef Kříž in 1927

The Czechoslovak Republic inherited a Prague surrounded by a ring of independent townships, and it soon carried out what the Austro-Hungarian government in Vienna had prevented for so long. In 1920 eight districts, eleven townships and twenty-six villages along the circumference were linked into Greater Prague, which thus became a Central European metropolis with a population of over 670,000. The entire Prague territory, which, since the Middle Ages, had served as the economic hinterland of the capital of Bohemia, finally became one administrative unit and in size Prague equalled, for example, Amsterdam.

With the establishment of Greater Prague in 1920 a State Regulation Commission was set up with the task of controlling the building up of the individual districts and working out a comprehensive territorial plan for the whole capital city. For the first time in history new modern town planning principles were applied, including scientific and artistic concerns and all the intricate questions of city life and the working environment, transport and leisure time facilities. Even if private ownership of the land and speculation of building contractors greatly complicated the work of the Commission, it did manage to put into practice progressive ideas and proposals for the reconstruction and building up of Prague as a large modern city.

An exemplary case of correctly understood and well-conceived town planning is the plan put forward by the architect Antonín Engel in 1912 for the building up of Dejvice. It was devised on a grand scale, incorporating the wide October Revolution Square (nám. Říjnové revoluce), the largest in Prague, broad streets, open areas of

The building of the Central Council of Trade Unions at Žižkov, originally the General Pensions Institute, the work of the architects Josef Havlíček and Karel Honzík, 1930—1932, the first high-rise building in Prague

The National Memorial on Vítkov Hill, built according to a plan by the architect Jan Zázvorka. Inside is the mausoleum of leading representatives of the country and of Soviet soldiers who liberated Prague in May 1945. In front of the building stands the bronze equestrian statue of Jan Žižka, the Hussite General, by Bohumil Kafka, 1950.

lawns and avenues of trees. Sufficient space was left for the complex of faculty buildings of the Czech University of Technology, added in the sixties of our century.

Remarkable plans for the building up of residential quarters were put forward for Spořilov and Ořechovka, where modern villas and family houses were located. One of the most successful was Baba, a colony of villas, designed by the architect Pavel Janák in 1928. Some of the leading modern Czech architects like Josef Gočár, Oldřich Starý and Ladislav Žák worked on the projects for individual houses.

In 1925—1929 Spořilov grew into a district of economical dwellings for office employees, following a plan of small family houses worked out by the architect Josef Bertl. The district of Ořechovka in Dejvice was, on the other hand, the first modern villa district in Prague. The Regulation Plan was elaborated in 1920 by the architect Jaroslav Vondrák and the individual designs are the work of Pavel Janák, Bohumír Kozák and Bohumil Hypšman as well as the famous pioneer of modern architecture Adolf Loos, whose villa for Dr. Müller is an outstanding example of Constructivism (1930).

Following the example of English garden cities, new comfortable villa districts with smaller family houses stretched in a broad band from the southern slopes of Strahov to the Vltava in the north-west. After 1927 Max Urban worked out a town plan for

Interior of the National Technical Museum at Letná,
built according to plans by the architect Milan
Babuška, 1938—1941

building up an extensive quarter south of Smíchov with villas and a coffee-house with a lighthouse tower, terraces and a swimming pool, which was given the name of the famous French geologist Barrande and called Barrandov. At its end stand the Czechoslovak State Film Studios, built in 1931—1933 likewise according to a project by Max Urban.

A strip of villas extended also on the right bank of the Vltava, stretching from the southern end of Vinohrady to Strašnice and north as far as Kobylisy. Apart from these villa colonies many tenement houses were built for workers in the industrial area of Vysočany with small flats lacking all conveniences.

Less successful was the construction of big buildings of ministries, central authorities and university faculties in inner Prague, for which space was reserved on empty sites along the banks of the river from Podskalí in the south as far as the present Šverma Bridge in the north. The regulation of the river with tall embankment walls destroyed the former picturesqueness of these parts, and the heavy mass of architecture prevented views into the charming little streets of the Old Town. Exemplary artistic treatment can only be found on some of the civic buildings below Emmaus Monastery near Palacký Bridge, built in 1924—1929 according to a project by Bohumil Hypšman. The individual buildings fit sensitively into the rising terrain of the town.

On the left bank of the Vltava the Regulation Commission managed, fortunately, to prevent the implementation of drastic plans, aimed at doing away with the Čertovka Stream and building a thoroughfare along the Lesser Town banks, thus destroying Kampa Island.

The twenties of our century enriched the most important and artistically highly sensitive place in the whole of Prague, Prague Castle, with remarkable new works. First, the palaces in the Castle were adapted as the official residence of the President of the Republic. This responsible task was successfully undertaken, on the wishes of the first President, T. G. Masaryk, by the Slovenian architect Josip Plečnik (1872—1957), who designed the present appearance of the first courtyard and the entrance to the official rooms of the festive stairway leading to Spanish Hall, the interior of the Golden Room in the Romanesque White Tower, the pavement of the third courtyard with the monolith of Mrákotín marble and the general layout of the surroundings of the Castle. Plečnik was assisted in this work by his disciple, the architect Otto Rotmayer (1892—1966).

An even more important undertaking was the Neo-Gothic completion of the metropolitan Cathedral of St Vitus, begun in 1873 according to a design by Josef Mocker but finished only in 1929, the thousandth anniversary of St Wenceslas. The financially demanding construction undertaking was completed only in the independent republic, which gave modern artists a chance to contribute to the monumental decorations. Stained glass windows were designed by Max Švabinský, Alfons Mucha, František Kysela and Karel Svolinský. The bronze door of the western portal was designed by

The Great Hall of the Carolinum, the Gothic 14th century hall adapted by the architect Jaroslav Frágner in 1946—1950. The tapestry with Charles IV before St Wenceslas was woven according to a carton by Vladimír Sychra, the statue of Charles IV is the work of the sculptor Karel Pokorný.

V. H. Brunner and modelled by Otakar Španiel. The busts in the triforium were made by Jan Štursa, Bohumil Kafka and Václav Žalud.

Even if the Neo-Gothic nave and aisles with the two towers on the façade is not the result of rare artistic consecration and its mass overpowered the Parlerian choir, it has grown so deep into our awareness of the Hradčany panorama that we cannot really imagine our view of Prague without it.

Constructivism, Functionalism and the Prague School of Modern Art

From the twenties on, Prague became a leading centre of Constructivist and Functionalist architecture and modern art in the world. The work of Jan Kotěra and the Cubist architects, before the First World War, prepared the way followed by the young generation of architects after the establishment of the Czechoslovak Republic.

Cubism died away in the decorative conception of what was known as Curvo-Linear Style, applied by Josef Gočár on the building of the Legiobank at Poříčí (1922) and by Pavel Janák on the building of the Riunione Adriatica Society at the corner of Národní and Jungmannova streets (1922). But there were already growing endeavours to move away from decorativeness and to stress function (The Hlava Pathological Institute and the Purkyně Physiological Institute at Albertov by Alois Špalek, 1920—1925).

The Institute of Macro-Molecular Chemistry of the Czechoslovak Academy of Sciences at Petřiny, designed by the architect Karel Prager in 1960—1964

The building of the Federal Assembly of the Czechoslovak Socialist Republic, built to a project by the architect Karel Prager et al., 1967—1973

After 1925 the first purely functional architecture went up (the Olympic Department Store by Jaromír Krejcar, 1926—1927, the Prague Trade Fair Palace — Veletržní palác — by Josef Fuchs and Oldřich Tyl, 1924—1928).

At the end of the twenties and in the thirties Functionalism and Constructivism prevailed in modern Prague architecture to such an extent that the capital of Czechoslovakia can, to this day, pride itself on the number of buildings erected. The Baťa Department Store on Wenceslas Square by the architect Ludvík Kysela (1929), the Headquarters of the Electricity Board of the Capital City of Prague near Hlávka Bridge by Adolf Benš and Josef Kříž (1935), and the House of Arts and Crafts on Národní street by Oldřich Starý (1935) are among the most successful examples.

Schools and sports stadiums were built in the Functionalist style, e.g. Strahov Stadium, one of the largest in the world, and the Winter Stadium on Štvanice Island (1934). They were followed by hospitals, Bulovka (1924—1934), the Military Hospital at Střešovice (1936), the Thomayer Hospital in Krč (1928), and by Ruzyně Airport (1933—1934). Then there were representative buildings of importance (the Memorial of National Liberation on Vítkov Hill by Jan Zázvorka, 1927—1932) and churches, e.g. St Wenceslas' (sv. Václav) in Vršovice by Josef Gočár (1928), and the Assembly of the Church of Czechoslovakia in Vinohrady by Pavel Janák (1932—1933).

Josip Plečnik designed the Church of the Most Sacred Heart of the Lord (Nejsvětější srdce Páně, 1927) on George of Poděbrady Square (nám. Jiřího z Poděbrad) in Vino-

Klement Gottwald Bridge across the Nusle Valley, built after a project by the architects V. Michálek and S. Hubička in 1965—1973

hrady, in bizarre originality related to Art Nouveau decorativeness, which strikingly differs from the terse form of other sacral buildings by the use of concrete.

The restrained architecture of the Memorial of National Liberation with its monumental size and the equestrian monument to Jan Žižka, on the whole, fit well into the appearance of the town. This cannot be said of the first high-rise building in Prague — the General Pensions Institute in Žižkov (1929—1934), which today is the headquarters of the Central Council of Trade Unions; its design by architect Josef Havlíček and Karel Honzík was highly functional but omitted to take into account its relation to the surroundings.

During the first Czechoslovak Republic the present appearance of the Golden Cross was completed; this is the crossing at the bottom of Wenceslas Square, Příkopy and 28. října streets leading to Národní street. The building of the National Museum had given a new scale to the whole of Wenceslas Square, where the low Renaissance and Baroque houses were replaced by department stores, hotels, buildings of publishing companies and printers. The department store with the Alfa Coffee House (L. Kysela and J. Jarolím, 1926—1928), Lindt House (1927) and Baťa House (1928—1929) both by L. Kysela, and Tatran Palace (P. Janák, 1932) show to this day the outstanding level of Prague Constructivist and Functionalist architecture. The former Cubist architects also participated in projects for new bridges. Pavel Janák worked on the bridge in Libeň (Libeňský most), the broadest and longest in Prague (1925—1928), Josef Chochol on what is today Barricade Fighters Bridge (most Barikádníků) in Troja (1926—1928), and Vlastislav Hofman on Jirásek Bridge (Jiráskův most) at the end of Resslova street (1933).

In the twenties and thirties Prague assumed an important place in European culture and became an attractive centre of modern literature and art. In the first half of the twenties the tone was set by Czech poets of proletarian poetry (Jiří Wolker, S. K. Neumann, Josef Hora, Jindřich Hořejší, and Jaroslav Seifert) with a counterpart in social painting and sculpture (painters Karel Holan, Miroslav Holý, Pravoslav Kotík, sculptors Jan Lauda, Karel Pokorný).

When Jiří Wolker died in 1924, proletarian poetry was replaced by Poetism, which substituted pure lyricism for social content and intensified the artistic effect of poetry. The Poetists — poets Vítězslav Nezval, Konstantin Biebl, Jaroslav Seifert — and theoretician Karel Teige wished to save for Man, depressed by modern civilization, natural feelings, power of imagination, joy of creation and delight in playfulness. Spontaneous lyricism was to offer people "all the beauty of the world". Its parallel in painting was Czech Lyrical Cubism (Emil Filla, Alois Wachsman, František Muzika) and the Artificialism of Jindřich Štýrský and Toyen (in 1927—1931), which vacillated between geometrical abstraction and Surrealism.

Poetism also took over the theatres in which an avant-garde position was held by Jiří Voskovec and Jan Werich in their Liberated Theatre (Osvobozené divadlo, after 1927) and by E. F. Burian in his D 34 Theatre.

In the thirties the most avant-garde of artists of all branches, including theoreticians who shared a Marxist approach, were associated in the Prague Surrealist Group (1934—1938). Alongside them there existed a broad range of other currents in art, with different conceptions and forms of expression, represented in a number of art unions, and allowing for individual differences.

Among prose writers greatest renown in the world during the First World War was won by Jaroslav Hašek with his *Good Soldier Schweik* and by Karel Čapek with his anti-war novels and plays. By their side worked a large number of poets, writers, painters, sculptors and composers, who each contributed to Prague growing into a centre of art of world standard.

I. P. Pavlov Station of Prague Metro, 1970—1974

The Building of the City

After March 1939 and during the Second World War Prague was an occupied town, the capital of the Protectorate of Bohemia and Moravia. A Protector of the Reich sat at Prague Castle and a German Mayor in the town hall, and they systematically carried out a policy of Germanization. The town was exposed to a war economy and increasing shortage of goods and food. The German occupiers punished the least signs of resistance very cruelly. After the students' demonstration on 15 November 1939 the Nazis closed all universities, nine students were executed and over a thousand sent to concentration camps. A major wave of repression arose after the assassination of Heydrich in May 1942, but this did not deter the resistance movement.

Prague was the last town to be abandoned by the Nazis, since fighting continued even after the signing of the capitulation. The May 5th Rising against the occupiers, when the people mounted barricades for four days, came to an end when Prague was liberated by the Soviet Army on 9 May 1945.

Liberated Prague became once again the capital city of the Czechoslovak Republic, but the political orientation of the country changed radically. The Communist Party won the first post-war elections, and in 1948 became the leading force in the country.

The Central National Committee of the Capital City of Prague, headed by Communist

Inter-Continental Hotel on Curie Square in the Old Town, built to a design by the architect K. Filsak in 1974

The building of Koospol Ltd. on Leninova street, built to a design by architects S. Franc, V. Fencl and J. Nováček, 1975—1977

Lord-Mayor Dr. Václav Vacek, first attended to removing the scars of the war, then set to dealing with the burning problems that had accumulated in the past. Prague was to be a socialist metropolis, and therefore had, by stages, to overcome the disastrous legacy of the second half of the 19th century, with insufficient and unsuitable housing conditions, an outdated road system and class distinctions between individual districts.

After 1960 the National Committee of the Capital City of Prague tried to set down the perspectives for the future development of the town with its rising population, continuing industrial production and the protection of historical and artistically valuable monuments and entire city quarters. Year by year the pollution of the atmosphere increased; there was a growing housing problem, and a basic solution was needed for the road network.

Prague kept growing. In 1960 its territory was extended to include Ruzyně and other settlements, in 1968, twenty-one villages in the surroundings were incorporated and thirty more in 1974. By 1961 Prague had a million inhabitants, and in that year a Central Board of the Chief Architect of the Capital City of Prague was set up. It was given the task of working out a plan for the capital according to the latest town planning principles with regard to the specific structure and aspects of the town's historical and artistic development.

One of the most important undertakings was housing construction. At first the builders were unable to satisfy even the most urgent demands for new flats. For that reason the building of small groups of dwellings was abandoned, and large housing developments were projected with all the necessary civic facilities. Most of the flats were built on these housing developments, and their growth on the outskirts of Prague has become a characteristic feature of post-war expansion of the capital city. The small housing projects with some 5,000 inhabitants were soon replaced by large units (15,000 inhabitants) and finally by vast housing developments with complex civic facilities for 90,000 inhabitants. Apart from the experimental housing estate at the Invalidovna in the midst of the town according to a design by Jiří Novotný, Josef Polák and Vojtěch Šalda, which has served since 1951, all other new housing developments were sited on the outskirts.

From the sixties on more attention was paid to the aesthetic standards of the new architecture on the housing developments and their harmonious setting in the landscape. The establishment of large housing projects changed the structure of population of the Prague suburbs. This shift in population and the rapid development of motorized transport needed new road networks and transport facilities. Beginning with the building of Šverma Bridge and the Letná Tunnel (1952) improvements to the network of roads were made in various places of the city, but a satisfactory solution will be provided only when the main thoroughfares as prolongations of the motorways are completed right across the city, providing the shortest route of transit.

Concert at St George's Basilica at Prague Castle held during the Prague Spring Music Festival

The exhibition of Bohemian Gothic Art in the Collections of the National Gallery at St George's Convent at Prague Castle

In 1954 the building of the North-South Thoroughfare was begun and in 1965—1973 a two-level bridge (Klement Gottwald Bridge) was built across the Nusle Valley according to a project by Vojtěch Michálek and Stanislav Hubička. In 1967 a decision was finally reached on the construction of the Prague underground railway, Prague Metro. The project foresees three main lines, of which two are already in operation.

Prague is an enormous treasure house of cultural, historical and artistic monuments, which need to be preserved for the future. The Prague Centre of the Care for Ancient Monuments and the Protection of Nature was set up to provide care for these premises, to carry out research and supervision during restoration work. Enormous funds have been earmarked for the protection and renovation of these buildings. Reconstruction work was undertaken on the Carolinum and the Bethlehem Chapel (Jaroslav Frágner, 1950—1953), Emmaus Monastery, Strahov Monastery (adapted as the Museum of National Literature), the Star Summer Palace at the White Mountain (Pavel Janák, 1945—1951, today the Alois Jirásek and Mikoláš Aleš Museum), palaces at Hradčany and in the Lesser Town, parts of Prague Castle and its Baroque gardens.

In 1971 the Government of the Czech Socialist Republic proclaimed the inner city of Prague a preservation area and fifteen important buildings were proclaimed National Cultural Monuments. St George's Convent at the Castle was adapted by the National Gallery to house its Collections of Old, mainly Gothic and Baroque Czech Art

The Palace of Culture, designed by architects J. Mayer, V. Ustohnal, A. Marek and J. Králík and built in 1969—1981. The interior was decorated by almost sixty leading Czechoslovak artists.

and Agnes' Convent in the Old Town for the Collection of 19th-Century Czech Painting. The Riding School of Prague Castle, the Wallenstein Riding School, the Ball-Games Court and the Belvedere in the Royal Garden have also been renovated for exhibition purposes.

From the sixties on, the inner city and the suburban parts witnessed the construction of buildings which, in design and apt location in the landscape or city environment, are a dignified continuation of the progressive traditions of modern Prague architecture. These include the swimming pool in Podolí (Richard Podzemný and Gustav Kuchař, 1965, sculptural decorations by Vladimír Janoušek and Miloš Chlupáč), the Sports Hall in Stromovka Park (V. Krásný et alia), the House of Fashion on Wenceslas Square (Josef Hrubý, 1954—1956), the House of Children's Books on Národní street (C. Franc et alia 1967—1973), the Czechoslovak Federal Assembly building (Karel Prager et alia, 1967—1973), the building of Czechoslovak Television at Kavčí Hory (Jindřich Holý, 1960—1970), the high-rise building of the Motokov Company at

Pankrác, the monumental Palace of Culture at the end of Klement Gottwald Bridge, and the New Stage of the National Theatre (1978—1983) to mention only the most important.

Since Prague became one of the centres of international tourism in the sixties, it proved essential that the number of hotels, catering establishments and shops be increased. In 1966 a skilfully located and functionally designed motel was opened in the suburb of Motol, the work of Jindřich Pulkrábek and Jana Šrámková. A year later, the Park-Hotel was completed in Holešovice, designed by Zdeněk Edel and Josef Lavička. The most successful incorporation into the appearance of the town and the best composition in volume, space and interior furnishings was achieved in the Inter-Continental Hotel, the work of Karel Filsak (1974).

After the Second World War sculpture gained in significance, and sculptors aimed at monumental expression. Sculpture was used in the decoration and adaptation of civic buildings (the V. I. Lenin Museum, the National Memorial at Žižkov), and in affixing memorial plaques and busts (Egon Erwin Kisch in Kožná street by Břetislav Benda, Franz Kafka in Kaprova street by Karel Hladák, Ema Destinová on the Lesser Town Square by Jan Simota). Statues and memorials in public places, on squares, along the embankments, avenues and in parks call to mind leading personalities of world and national history.

Classical works of the post-war period include the Božena Němcová monument by Karel Pokorný on Slavonic Island (1952—1954), the Jan Hus monument by Karel Lidický in the courtyard of the Carolinum (1958) and the statue by Vincenc Makovský depicting the New Era, which stands in front of the Federal Assembly building (1957—1958) and symbolizes the onset of a new epoch in human history.

The Red Hill Housing Development and Leninova street at night

On a number of Prague housing developments modern sculpture embellishes the environment and improves the general appearance with its expressive and technical potentialities, ranging from figures to abstract shapes, and from classical to new materials.

At the present time Prague is the most important centre of scientific, cultural and artistic life in the entire country. Much admired among the towns of Europe and greatly visited for its beauty and art treasures, it is host to innumerable international congresses and symposia, whose participants are offered a wide variety of theatre performances, concerts and exhibitions. Greatest response is reaped by the annual Prague Spring Music Festival, which is a continuation of the great music tradition in the town.

The panorama of Prague from Letná

Modern Prague architecture has continued its logical development since the sixties, after certain deviations and obvious mistakes in the fifties. In the last few decades in particular it provides one of the interesting features of cultural life in Czechoslovakia's capital city on a par with modern Czech music and other arts. At the end of the fifties, for example, new ideas were put forward for a combination of several art forms and gave rise to the Magic Lantern and multi-screen film shows.

At the present time we are more conscious than ever that the Prague Basin is a historic and aesthetic unit where, through the centuries, art has co-operated with technology and nature to mould its structure. The builders of the little Romanesque churches and the Gothic cathedrals and the architects of Prague Baroque knew well that their work shaped the town into an organism where natural conditions — in the first place the terrain — could not be overcome by force but had to be made suitable use of.

For that reason only such architecture is acceptable that fits harmoniously and aesthetically into the cityscape. For nature in its balanced counterpoint of hills on the left bank and flat land on the right bank of the Vltava prepared a magnificent building site, such as can be found in few other cities in Europe. Each new building must, therefore, pay respect to this natural balance of the city image so that inconsiderate interference in the given hierarchy of spatial values should not upset what has been created in the course of the past one thousand years.

Prague, a modern city that incorporates clear marks of the Romanesque town and characteristic features of the Gothic and the Baroque town, is not simply a well-preserved memorial to the development of architecture and town planning. It is a living and growing capital city, which serves the present and the future, and now, as in the past, the most important events in the history of the whole country take place here.

For that reason the architects are not only maintaining and restoring important and valuable buildings belonging to the historical and artistic heritage. They are erecting new buildings that correspond to present-day views of life and our contemporary requirements. They have been given freedom to express themselves fully so that their work might help shape the new style of art of the near future, but they can do so only if due respect is paid to the work of their predecessors. This is particularly true of Prague, whose image was shaped by a pleiad of important local and foreign architects, who showed understanding for the given conditions and the artistic order arising from these and augmented and emphasized them in their work.

As long as contemporary architects respect the historical and artistic character of the town, it will be a guarantee that despite all the losses of monuments damaged, impoverished and interfered with in Prague in the last and in our own century, the city will remain in the future, too, one of the most artistically remarkable on a European and a world scale.

Index

Square brackets indicate location, parentheses specify subject

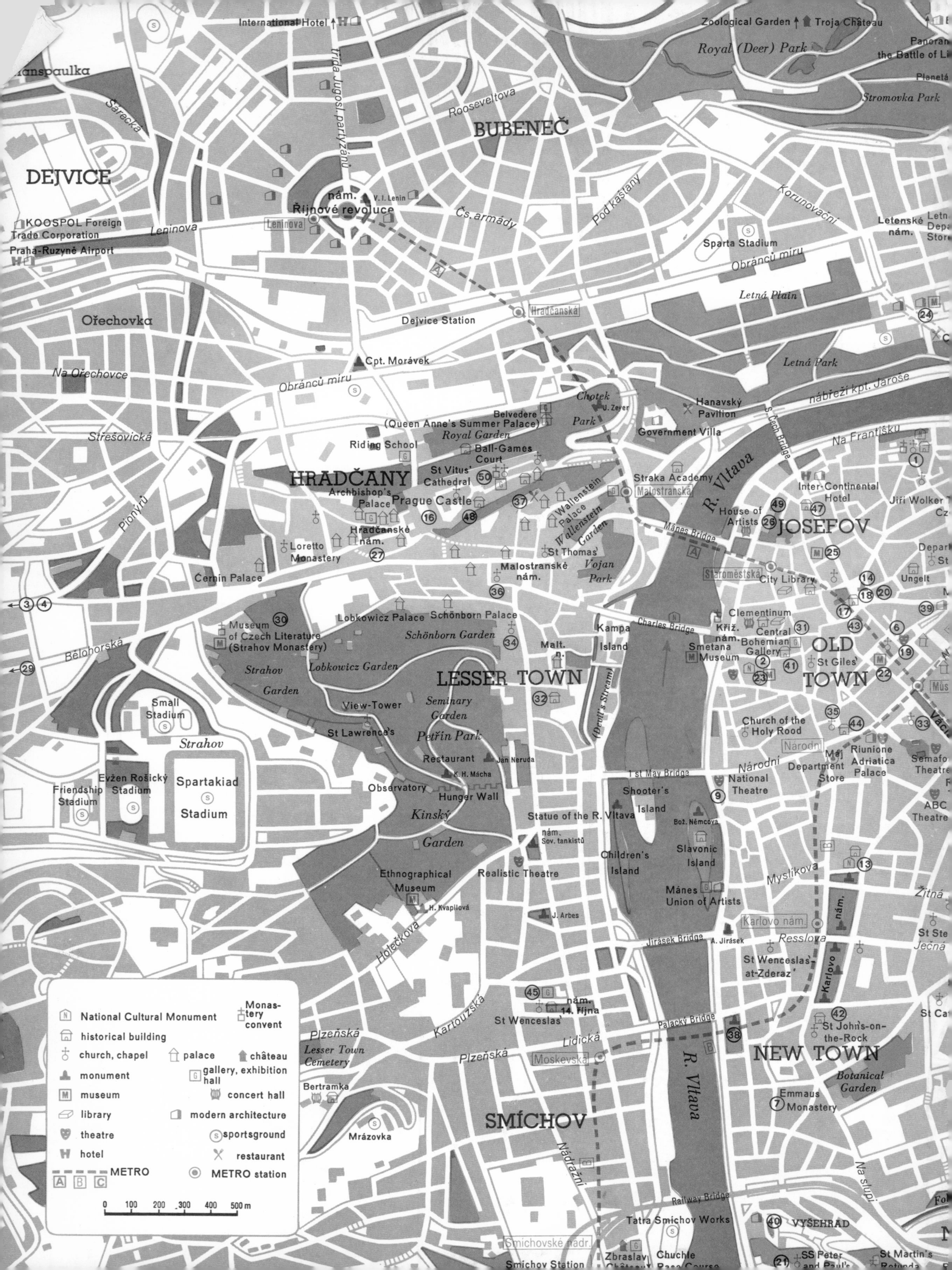
International Hotel
Zoological Garden
Troja Château
Royal (Deer) Park
Stromovka Park
třída Jugosl. partyzánů
Šárecká
Roosveltova
BUBENEČ
DEJVICE
nám. Říjnové revoluce
V. I. Lenin
Leninova
KOOSPOL Foreign Trade Corporation
Praha-Ruzyně Airport
Čs. armády
Pod kaštany
Korunovační
Letenské nám.
Sparta Stadium
Obránců míru
Letná Plain
Hradčanská
Dejvice Station
Ořechovka
Cpt. Morávek
Letná Park
Na Ořechovce
Obránců míru
Chotek Park
U. Zeyer
Hanavský Pavilion
nábřeží kpt. Jaroše
Belvedere (Queen Anne's Summer Palace)
Royal Garden
Government Villa
S. Čech Bridge
Na Františku
Střešovická
Riding School
Ball-Games Court
HRADČANY
St Vitus' Cathedral
Straka Academy
R. Vltava
Inter-Continental Hotel
Jiří Wolker
Archbishop's Palace
Prague Castle
Malostranská
Wallenstein Palace
Wallenstein Garden
House of Artists
JOSEFOV
Pionýrů
Hradčanské nám.
Mánes Bridge
Loretto Monastery
St Thomas'
Vojan Park
Malostranské nám.
Staroměstská
City Library
Ungelt
Černín Palace
Clementinum
Lobkowicz Palace
Schönborn Palace
Charles Bridge
Kříž. nám.
Museum of Czech Literature (Strahov Monastery)
Schönborn Garden
Kampa Island
Malt. n.
Smetana Museum
Central Bohemian Gallery
OLD TOWN
St Giles'
Bělohorská
Strahov Garden
Lobkowicz Garden
LESSER TOWN
Small Stadium
View-Tower
Seminary Garden
(Devil's Stream)
Church of the Holy Rood
St Lawrence's
Petřín Park
Strahov
Národní
Restaurant
Jan Neruda
1st May Bridge
Máj Department Store
Riunione Adriatica Palace
Evžen Rošický Stadium
Spartakiad Stadium
Friendship Stadium
K. H. Mácha
Shooter's Island
National Theatre
Observatory
Hunger Wall
Statue of the R. Vltava
Kinský Garden
nám. Sov. tankistů
Bož. Němcová
ABC Theatre
Children's Island
Slavonic Island
Myslíkova
Ethnographical Museum
Realistic Theatre
Mánes Union of Artists
H. Kvapilová
J. Arbes
Karlovo nám.
Hološkova
Jirásek Bridge
A. Jirásek
Resslova
St Wenceslas'-at-Zderaz
Karlovo nám.
Kartouzská
nám. 14. října
St Wenceslas'
Palacký Bridge
St John's-on-the-Rock
Plzeňská
Lesser Town Cemetery
Lidická
Plzeňská
Moskevská
NEW TOWN
Botanical Garden
Bertramka
Emmaus Monastery
SMÍCHOV
Mrázovka
Nádražní
Na slupi
Railway Bridge
Tatra Smíchov Works
VYŠEHRAD
Smíchovské nádr.
Smíchov Station
Zbraslav
Chuchle
SS Peter and Paul's
St Martin's
National Cultural Monument
Monastery convent
historical building
church, chapel
palace
château
monument
gallery, exhibition hall
museum
concert hall
library
modern architecture
theatre
sportsground
hotel
restaurant
METRO
METRO station
A B C
0 100 200 300 400 500 m